CImA

PUBLISHING

Better Exam Results

A Guide for Accountancy and Business Students

Samuel A. Malone

ELSEVIER

AMSTERDAM   BOSTON   HEIDELBERG   LONDON   NEW YORK   OXFORD
PARIS   SAN DIEGO   SAN FRANCISCO   SINGAPORE   SYDNEY   TOKYO

CIMA Publishing
An imprint of Elsevier
Linacre House, Jordan Hill, Oxford OX2 8DP
30 Corporate Drive, Burlington, MA 01803

First published 2005

British Library Cataloguing in Publication Data
A catalogue record for this book is available from the British Library

ISBN 0 7506 6357 X

For information on all CIMA publications visit our website at
www.cimapublishing.com

Typeset by Newgen Imaging Systems (P) Ltd., Chennai, India
Printed and bound in Great Britain

**Working together to grow
libraries in developing countries**

www.elsevier.com | www.bookaid.org | www.sabre.org

ELSEVIER   BOOK AID
             International   Sabre Foundation

Contents

About the author

Samuel Malone is an Associate of the Chartered Institute of Management Accountants, an Associate of the Institute of Chartered Secretaries and Administrators, a Member of the Institute of Industrial Engineers and a Fellow of the Irish Institute of Training and Development. He holds a Masters degree in Education from the University of Sheffield. He is a well-known author and training consultant, and has a particular interest in learning skills.

Preface

Learning is a verb, not a noun.
It's a journey – not a destination.

This book has been particularly written with the accountancy and business student in mind. Whether you are a full-time student, a part-time student, a correspondence course student, a practising manager who wants to improve and develop himself, or indeed anybody interested in developing learning-to-learn skills, this book is for you. It will give you the latest findings on learning and brain research and show you how to organize for studying, make notes, read faster and more effectively, improve memory, maximize performance in the examination room, and improve learning and problem-solving skills generally.

Most people get no formal training in study and exam skills, and yet students with such training consistently do better in examinations than students without this knowledge. Study skills or learning-to-learn skills are not the sole preserve of students, as learning is a lifelong process. Technology is advancing at a very rapid rate, and most people will change careers a number of times in a single lifetime. As a result they will be confronted with new experiences and learning situations; for example, many managers on taking up new positions undertake informal studies and reading programmes to help them understand their new roles more adequately, while others are sent on formal off-the-job training and development courses.

The more ambitious pursue formal studies in such areas as accountancy, administration, marketing, purchasing, personnel, industrial engineering, computer science, transport and so on. Some people even undertake formal professional and university degrees in their third and fourth decades while holding down a responsible job and running a family home. Even university graduates on taking up employment often find it necessary to pursue professional qualifications and other postgraduate studies if they want to progress into middle and top management positions.

All these people need to develop learning-to-learn skills. More is now known about the brain's learning potential and how people learn than ever before. Such knowledge is now available in this book and can be used to improve your learning ability. Don't rely on hearsay, old wives' tales and an unsystematic approach to learning; apply the systematic approach outlined in this book, now!

This version of a previous publication titled *Learning to Learn* has been substantially revised and expanded. New chapters on Learning about learning (Chapter 1) and Reports/assignments and dissertation (Chapter 9) have been included, while Chapters 7 and 12, on Case studies and Examination technique respectively, have been updated and expanded.

Samuel A. Malone

Acknowledgements

Tony Buzan is the creator of Mind Maps. The term 'Mind Map' is the copyright of Tony Buzan.

The author would also like to acknowledge the inventor of the SQ3R Method, Professor R. P. Robinson.

Every attempt has been made to trace and acknowledge copyright material. The author and publisher will be happy to acknowledge copyright in future editions.

1

Learning about learning

They know enough who know how to learn
Henry Adams

Learning objectives

- What does L = P + Q mean?
- What is the difference between deep and surface learning?
- What is the learning cycle and learning styles?
- What are the stages of learning?
- How does the brain facilitate learning?
- How do adult learners learn?

Introduction

It is useful for students to know something about learning and how the brain facilitates learning. When you buy a computer, you are given an instruction manual on how it works. However, very few students get any instruction on how their brain works, despite the fact that it is the most powerful computer on earth. This chapter will give a brief overview of some key developments in brain and learning research that will help you become a better student.

What is learning?

Reg Revan formulated a simple model of learning: L = P + Q. This means that learning equals programmed knowledge plus the ability to ask incisive questions. As an accountant you will learn a whole range of principles, rules, theories, specialist knowledge and techniques relating to the profession of accountancy. This part of your studies can be thought as the programmed learning. Although a good memory is the foundation for all knowledge, it is particularly needed for this type of learning.

However, in addition to the whole system of codified accounting knowledge you must learn, you will need to develop problem-solving skills, powers of analysis, synthesis, judgement, insight and creativity. These are the type of skills needed to be successful as an accountant, and are developed through your studies and on-the-job training. In fact, under the new syllabus, practical experience requirements for CIMA include communication skills, negotiation skills, interpersonal relationship skills and the management of people.

Accountancy is not just about dealing with programmed problems; you will also be confronted with unprogrammed problems, which will need good problem-solving skills, initiative and insight to find a solution. Most of the programmed knowledge you will need as an accountant is examined in the earlier stages of your examinations. These exams are often assessed using multiple choice and computer-based assessment. This is where good memory techniques are most useful.

The final stages of your examinations are designed to test your ability in problem-solving, conceptualization, comprehension, integration, interpretation, analysis, synthesis, application and evaluation. These stages of the professional accountancy exams test your higher cognitive skills rather than rote memory. Another useful idea in learning is to know the difference between deep learning and surface learning.

Deep versus surface learning

Deep learning is what you need to do to gain understanding and insight, to see relationships between information, to question what you read, and to draw conclusions from the evidence given. Surface learning is mere rote memorization without any regard to meaning and understanding.

As students, many of you will have gone through an education system that emphasized examination success through memorization and the regurgitation of information. The objective was to get through exams rather than really understand what you were learning. Consequently, the information learned was quickly forgotten as soon as you completed the exams. However, a different approach to learning is needed to pass university and professional exams, particularly at the final stages.

Deep learners display the following characteristics:

- They have a strong desire to understand the subject – it is easier to remember a subject that you understand and make sense of
- They critically interact with the subject by asking questions and seeking answers
- They relate the subject matter to their prior knowledge and experience; this linking and associating imprints the information in their memory
- They organize ideas to see relationships and underlying patterns
- They make sure that conclusions drawn are supported by adequate evidence
- They examine the logic of conclusions in relation to common sense.

Surface learners display the following characteristics:

- They memorize facts and procedures without regard to underlying principles
- They passively accept ideas and information without question
- They have no learning plan or strategy
- They fail to see underlying principles and patterns

- They are driven by a desire to pass the exam rather than understand the topic
- They are satisfied with reproducing information rather than making it their own through reorganization and reflection.

From a student's perspective, your approach should be always to understand what you are studying rather than learning by rote. Surface learning may get you through the earlier stages of your course but is unlikely to get you through the final stages, where you need to show the higher skills of conceptualization, analysis, synthesis and problem-solving. At university, case studies, assignments and dissertations are designed to test deep learning. In the CIMA, the case study in the final stages of the exam is uniquely designed to test this type of learning.

Learning cycle and learning styles

The learning cycle is to do something, reflect on it, conclude and do something differently. We learn by reflecting on our experiences, making conclusions and applying what we've learned by doing something differently. This is how we learn from our mistakes. Similarly, students should learn from their experiences, by drawing conclusions and applying what they have learned to other situations. Accountancy students should be continually looking for opportunities to apply their academic knowledge to practical work situations.

There is no agreement on learning styles, as there are various ways of looking at the styles people use when learning. One particular approach is based on the senses. Students prefer a particular medium when learning – some like to learn by watching, others like to learn by listening, while others like to learn by doing. This is called visual, auditory and kinaesthetic learning. We all use a combination of the three styles, but most of us have a preference for one style over the others.

Learning styles can also be based on the learning cycle. Doing something is called the activist style, reflecting is called the reflector style, concluding is called the theorist style, while doing something different is called the pragmatic style.

Students with an activist style prefer a hands-on approach, such as using case studies, simulations and role-play. Students with a reflector style like to listen to lectures and to review and reflect on what was said. Students with a theorist style like concepts, models, principles and theories. Students with a pragmatist style like to try things out in practice to see if they work; they like project work, assignments and action plans.

Learning styles can also be based on context. Some students like to work on their own, some like to work in small groups, while others like to work in large groups. For example, it takes a particular type of student to be comfortable with a correspondence course or e-learning, and hence the drop-out rate for such programmes is very high. Most of us prefer the company of others, which we can get by attending classes and working in groups.

There are tests you can take to determine your learning style. Peter Honey and Alan Mumford have designed a learning styles questionnaire which you can take to determine your learning style. It is easy to do and only takes about 20 minutes. Most people have a mix of the four styles with a preference for a particular style.

As a student, you should ascertain what particular learning preferences you have. If you know your particular preference, then you can do something to strengthen your abilities in the other styles. Some students may have a weak reflector style, which means they do not think or reflect deeply enough on issues, but you need to reflect on topics if you want to really understand and remember them. Different learning styles can influence the outcome of learning. As a student, you should discover the learning style that optimizes your learning.

Stages of learning

Students go through four stages when learning:

(1)   *Unconscious incompetence.* This is the stage when you are not aware of what you don't know. Before they study accountancy students have no idea of what is involved and the effort, time and dedication it takes to qualify as an accountant. Many don't realize the variety of subjects, in addition to accounting, that they have to sit – such as economics, law, management, information technology, taxation and so on. On qualifying, it will take another few years before you are a master of the art. Right now you are just unaware of your level of ignorance and lack of experience as regards accountancy.

(2)   *Conscious incompetence.* This is the stage of learning when you realize the extent of how much you don't know. You have started learning accountancy and, because of the size of the workload involved and the perceived difficulty of the task, it seems like an impossible task. This is the novice stage, and it is important not to get discouraged. Motivation, goals, action plans, persistence and taking responsibility for your own learning will see you there in the end.

(3)   *Conscious competence.* This is the stage where you are proficient in accounting but not a master of the art. You have still to think through very carefully what you're doing all the time. It takes all your concentration and energy to get your work done on time and to a satisfactory standard.

(4)   *Unconscious competence.* At this stage you are master of the art of accounting. At work your unconscious mind can take over the routine, freeing your mind to concentrate on the more difficult aspects of accounting. You can do most work in automatic mode. As a student you can arrive at this stage through overlearning subjects. Overlearning makes students exam proficient in their subjects, and this is why students when preparing for exams are often recommended to overlearn key topics. This enables them to react automatically under stressful examination conditions.

The brain and learning

The following are some useful facts about how the brain facilitates learning:

- The brain expands with use. The more we learn, the more connections and interconnections are laid down in the brain.
- Experience is the best teacher. Physical movement is regulated by the cerebellum, which stores skill memory. This type of memory is particularly long lasting. This is why, once

learnt, we never forget how to ride a bicycle or swim. This highlights the importance for accountancy students of actually doing accounting problems rather than just reading about them. Practice lays down permanent pathways in the brain.

- The brain is a patterned phenomenon. It learns by linking and making associations. Learning is maximized by integrating the left logical side of the brain with the right creative side.
- Emotions influence the strength of learning. Feelings and emotions as well as thinking are part of the learning process. The more excitement, enthusiasm, confidence and self-belief you put in to your learning, the greater the strength and permanency of the learning. Positive feelings enhance learning, whereas negative feelings inhibit learning. Severe stress is a barrier to learning. People are more receptive to learning when they are relaxed. Students should adopt relaxation techniques as part of their strategic approach to learning.
- The human brain has a visual cortex that is five times larger than the auditory cortex. This is probably why visual learning is so effective. When learning, students should engage the visual senses as much as possible.
- About 90 per cent of the brain's mass is water. Students should drink sufficient water when studying to ensure their brains do not become dehydrated.
- Active imagination and visualization enhance learning. The brain is an image processor rather than a word processor. It cannot distinguish between mental rehearsal and actually doing it, which is why students should visualize and mentally rehearse information that they need to learn. Positive affirmations can reinforce the process.

Multiple IQ

Until Howard Gardner came along with his theory of multiple intelligences, academics viewed intelligence from a very limited perspective. They measured intelligence in terms of verbal and mathematical abilities, and people who scored badly in these tests were considered to be unintelligent. In Gardner's more sophisticated model, people have the following mix of intelligences in greater or lesser amounts:

- *Spatial.* People with spatial intelligence like objects and shapes, charts, designs, diagrams, pictures and maps. They like to draw, design and create things. Accountants with this ability would be good at flowcharting, and converting statistical tables into graphs, pie charts and bar charts. Student accountants can get extra marks for illustrating their answers in exams with appropriate models and diagrams.
- *Interpersonal.* This is part of emotional intelligence. There is no doubt but that technical skills will only get an accountant so far in his or her career. Successful accountants need to be able to influence other people, operate in teams, resolve conflicts and negotiate effectively.
- *Intrapersonal.* This is another aspect of emotional intelligence, and is the ability to reflect on issues and increase our understanding of events. People with intrapersonal intelligence have a high level of self-understanding. They know their own strengths and weaknesses, motivations, interests, goals and feelings. It is very difficult to understand others if you do not understand yourself. Reflection, gaining insights and understanding is an essential skill for the professional and student accountant alike.

- *Musical.* The enjoyment of music can be a good way for busy accountants to relax in their spare time, as a way of unwinding and getting rid of the stresses of the day. Student accountants can study with baroque music playing gently in the background to invoke a state of relaxation and enhance learning.
- *Linguistic.* This is an ability with words and self-expression. To succeed in your career, you need to be able to express yourself orally and in writing. Good presentation skills such as public speaking and report-writing skills are essential in your work as an accountant. As a student accountant written presentation skills are tested at various stages of the exams, including report-writing skills.
- *Mathematical.* A substantial part of the accountancy course is designed to test your analytical and mathematical skills. Subjects like costing, management accounting, financial management and business mathematics test your logical and mathematical skills. Other subjects, like law and information technology, demand a high level of analytical ability.
- *Kinaesthetic.* Accountancy is a hands-on skill, and to become proficient in it you need a good deal of practice. It would be impossible to pass accountancy exams without plenty of practice at doing past questions. You should compare your attempts with the recommended solutions, see where you went wrong, take corrective action, and make sure that if a similar question came up in the future you would not make the same mistake.

Adult learners

Many people come to the accountancy profession with relevant university qualifications and earn exemptions from some of the exams. Many have acquired considerable work experience by this stage. In fact, they are adult learners and therefore think like adult learners. So how do adult learners think? In a learning situation, adult learners operate from the following perspectives:

- They are independent and self-directed. They like to be in control and take responsibility for their own learning.
- Because they have experience, they like opportunities to display and use this experience. They actively try to link academic knowledge to their prior experience.
- They are motivated by goals, and like to know the reason why they are learning something.
- They like to solve problems and to learn things that they will be able to use in practice to further their work ambitions and careers. This gives learning a purpose and focus. Adults respond better to problem-based courses than to lectures.
- Adults like frequent feedback on how they are doing so that they can learn from inappropriate methods and mistakes.
- They like a supportive learning environment with a lecturer who acts like a facilitator rather than a teacher.
- They like to be challenged just beyond their comfort zone to keep their motivation up. Too much challenge may make them feel discouraged and out of their depth. Just the right amount of challenge keeps them interested and alert.

Summary

A useful definition of learning is L = P + Q, where L stands for learning, P for programmed learning, and Q for the ability to ask incisive questions. Deep learning is what you need to do to gain understanding and insight, to see relationships between information, to question what you read, and to draw conclusions from the evidence provided. Surface learning is mere rote memorization without regard to meaning and understanding.

The learning cycle is to do something, reflect on it, conclude and do something differently. Students should realize that reflection is a very important aspect of learning.

There are different ways of looking at learning styles. One way is to concentrate on the senses, such as visual, auditory and kinaesthetic. Another way is to consider styles such as activist, reflector, theorist and pragmatist. Although we possess all the styles, we each have a preference for some styles over others. Becoming aware of our particular learning style will make us aware of our shortcomings and encourage us to develop strengths in the other styles.

The four stages of learning are unconscious incompetence, conscious incompetence, conscious competence and, finally, unconscious competence. Students must go through these to become masters of accounting.

Knowing how the brain facilitates learning should improve our ability to learn more effectively. Use it or lose it. The brain expands with use, and should be exercised by continuous learning just like any other muscle in the body. Experience is the best teacher and visual learning is particularly powerful.

The theory of multiple IQ gives a new perspective on how diverse our intelligence is. Accountants need all the intelligences in one way or another. It is no longer sufficient just to be good at numbers to be a successful accountant. Emotional intelligence in the form of interpersonal and intrapersonal is very important.

By the time most people come to studying professional accountancy, they are in their early- or mid-twenties. They are in fact adults and think like adults. Adult learners have certain characteristics which students of accountancy should be aware of, and these are discussed in the chapter so that students become more aware of how they learn.

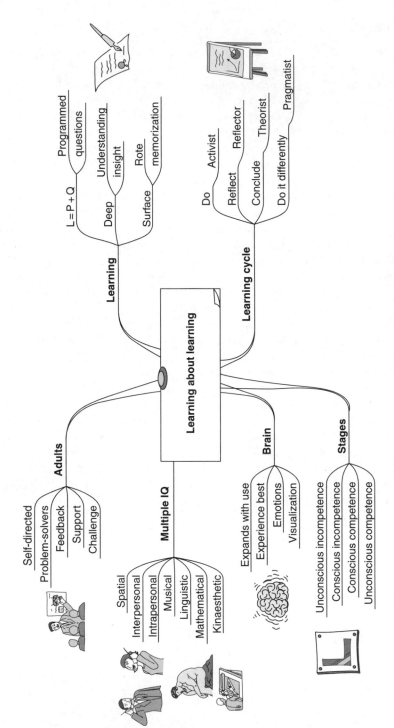

Mind Map of Chapter 1: Learning about learning

Organizing your study

The secret of success is constancy to purpose.
Benjamin Disraeli

Learning objectives

- How do I plan and organize my study?
- How much time should I spend studying?
- Why should I use a timetable?

Motivation

Without the proper motivation and determination to succeed, undertaking a difficult course of study such as a university degree or professional qualification can be a waste of time. Such courses require a strong commitment of time and energy, and a will to succeed. If you feel you lack this commitment, most educationalists would advise you not to proceed any further. Perhaps you could use your time more productively on a less demanding programme in the same area.

Self-confidence is the first requisite to great undertakings. To succeed in your studies, you must be confident. The more successful you are, the more confident you become in your studies and examinations. One reinforces the other.

Confidence and motivation are also interlinked. The importance of motivation cannot be overemphasized. Motivation can be derived from within yourself – such as the desire to achieve for achievement's sake – and internal motivation is the most powerful driver. Motivation may also be derived from external sources, such as the need for social approval, the desire for higher remuneration or the need to keep up with your peers.

Interest in a subject also has a very strong positive motivational effect on learning and improves your capacity to learn. On the other hand, dislike for a subject has a negative motivational effect on learning. Whatever the source of your motivation, the diligent plodder often succeeds where the brilliant but lazy student fails. Thus, low levels of motivation can result in poor academic performance even in very able people.

Planning

Mnemonics, which are specially designed sets of associations, help to give organization to otherwise unconnected material. Such mnemonic techniques include the use of rhymes, imagery and association. They will help you in your studies, especially with remembering factual material such as terms, definitions, key points and theories. However, they are less useful where higher intellectual processes such as comprehension, application, analysis, synthesis and evaluation are involved. Nevertheless, they will give you a firm foundation on which to build and develop these processes.

One such mnemonic is **PASS**. This is easy to remember for obvious reasons. **P** stands for Plan, **A** for Attention, **S** for Set Time and **S** for Systematic. Now let's look at each of these.

Plan

Planning is just as important to you in your studies as it is in business. Planning includes setting objectives and measuring actual performance against targets. For study purposes, just as in business, it can be conveniently subdivided into four categories:

1. *Strategic.* Strategic plans and objectives are for up to five years ahead. Your strategic objective may, for example, be: 'I want to become a qualified accountant in four years'. Sub-objectives would be to complete each stage of the examination in one year.

2. *Tactical.* Tactical plans and objectives cover the period for up to one year. Study the examination syllabus carefully. Ensure that your texts, study packs and correspondence school notes cover the syllabus adequately. Have a programme of studies mapped out week by week and month by month, and keep a chart monitoring your actual rate of progress against your plan. Success in keeping to your objectives will strengthen your motivation.

3. *Operational.* These are your day-to-day plans and objectives. Always set down an objective before you get down to each study session. This objective should be as concrete as possible – for instance, you may set yourself the task of memorizing certain key definitions essential for success in the examination. On the other hand, you may set yourself the objective of understanding some concept in accountancy, or you may want to get through a chapter and be able to answer satisfactorily the sample examination questions at the end.

4. *Progress monitoring.* Comparing your actual progress against your objectives at each of the three levels is most important. Corrective action to remedy shortcomings should be taken to put your studies back on target again. Self-testing and answering tests set by your tutor should be part of your strategy.

Attention

Always focus your attention on the task at hand. Daydreaming must be eliminated if you are to succeed. When attending lectures, pay attention to what is being said. Listening is a skill that improves with practice. As you listen to the lecturer try to summarize the key points in your mind, and on paper by making brief notes or using keywords. In general, adopt an attitude of paying attention to detail in all things.

Set time

Have set time for work and also for recreation. Time management is all important if you are to succeed in your studies. Naturally this is going to be inconvenient and will interfere with your leisure pursuits, but if you want to succeed you must plan your time in the form of a timetable. Also put time aside for recreation. The old saying 'all work and no play makes Jack a dull boy' should not be forgotten.

Systematic

This means being methodical in your approach and working in accordance with your plan. So be systematic in all things, especially in your study. Acquire a habit and routine of studying to such an extent that if you are not studying when you should be, you feel guilty about it.

Study time

Study time is often a stumbling block. How much time should you devote to study? Studying for a degree or professional qualification, especially on a part-time basis, is not an easy task. However, the task will be made more manageable if you are prepared to give it sufficient study time.

Professional accountancy examinations usually consist of three to four stages. For example, the CIMA consists of Foundation, Intermediate and Final Stages. This is due to change in 2005. As a part-time student beginning the exams, you could set yourself the objective of passing one stage every 18 months, completing the examinations in four to five years. Less time is needed to complete the examinations if you have obtained exemptions.

The time commitment to studying needs to be in the region of 16 to 20 hours per week. This assumes that you are studying on your own by correspondence course. A different profile is needed if you are attending lectures; here, 20 hours devoted to studying and attending lectures would seem reasonable. However, it is impossible to be too dogmatic about this and you should have regard to your own particular abilities and needs.

Remember, these are just targets. Be prepared for setbacks! Most people who sit professional examinations have to repeat one or more parts. Don't let setbacks knock you off your stride; just keep in mind that ordinary talent and extraordinary perseverance often see people through in the end. Analyse the reasons for your failure and learn from your mistakes. Be more prepared, preferably by having contingency plans, and so more resolved for your next attempt.

Of course, there can be other setbacks to your planned study programme due to events such as bereavement, sickness, changes in job circumstances (current or new) or domestic circumstances, or just plain lack of finance.

Study time availability analysis

You may well be asking at this stage, 'where will I get all this time for studying?' Well, let's suppose that you put Saturday and Sunday aside for recreation. How much time have you available for studying? Keep a diary for a few weeks to see exactly how you spend your time.

You should have at least 20 hours for study, assuming you use 40 hours for sleep, 40 hours for work, 10 hours for meals and 10 hours for travelling. However, it may be necessary to devote a few hours to revision on Saturdays coming up towards the examination.

Remember, these are just suggestions. It may suit you better to study during the week and over weekends, with mid-week breaks.

Timetables

The advantage of a study timetable is that it cuts out the necessity of deciding how to allocate your time whenever you get down to do a study session. It will also help you to stick to your plan.

Basically, there are two types of timetable that you should construct. Have a long-term plan for the year ahead, and for day-to-day working a flexible weekly timetable is needed. In addition, a specific list of learning objectives should be written for each study session. For example, at the end of the study session you should be able to display knowledge, in writing, that you did not possess before.

Carry your timetable around with you in a notebook. Until you have decided on a firm timetable, look at it each day. Plan your studies on a daily basis and set down your learning objectives. After a few weeks of experimentation, compile a firm timetable.

Revise your timetable from time to time on the basis of experience, preference or social requirements. However, as time goes on it will tend to become firmer as you disengage from other commitments. You may wish to spend more time on difficult subjects or to make up for study time unavoidably lost. One last word: remember to allow time in your timetable for revision and correspondence school tests, for reflection and consolidation of information are also important.

Designing the timetable

When drawing up a timetable, take the following points into consideration:

1. Decide on the number of hours for study each week.
2. Space the hours over the week. Remember to leave at least one day per week free for recreation.
3. Decide on the time of day for study. People with jobs usually have only evenings and weekends, but even so an hour's study in the morning before leaving for work may be worth more than its equivalent at night-time because the mind may be fresher. However, if you are one of those people who never reaches peak mental performance before 11 am, then morning study is not for you!
4. Decide how you will divide your time over the various subjects, allocating extra time to the subjects you find most difficult or you like least. These are the very subjects that could cost you the examination. Tackle these subjects first, when you are at your freshest, rather than later.
5. Decide on the length of each study session. Psychologists have found that optimum study efficiency is maintained if the sessions are of about 45 minutes' duration, followed by a five-minute period of recall and then by a five-minute period of rest. For the latter it is a good idea to get up and walk around (out in the fresh air for a few minutes, if possible).
6. Have variety in your timetable. A change of subject will refresh the mind.

Organizing and monitoring study sessions

It is said that efficient business people always start the day with a list of objectives to be achieved. Take a leaf from their book and be as specific as possible in what you plan to have achieved at the end of study sessions. Definite goals, in conjunction with your timetable, should give study sessions organization and purpose.

After the sessions, compare what you have actually learned with the learning objectives set. Knowledge of results and continuous feedback are important principles of effective learning.

Monitoring your progress will ensure that you are meeting the targets of your plan. Go back and study areas you don't really know; this will ensure that you do not 'jump ahead' without knowing the material you are currently studying. Most subjects are structured on a building-block basis, so premature jumping ahead will lead to confusion.

Each study session should be of about one hour's duration. Each evening might consist of three study sessions each devoted to a different subject, if possible. Begin each study session with a five-minute review of the previous night's work, and towards the end have a five-minute review of this session's work.

Use the last five minutes of each study session for a break. Get up, stretch, and walk about. It is a good idea to do a few physical exercises to keep your blood flowing, such as sit-ups, tipping your toes and so on. This will keep your body supple and your mind alert.

Getting started

Getting started is often a problem. Remember the saying that procrastination is the thief of time, and start actively studying straight away. Spending the first five minutes of each study session reviewing what you last studied on the subject is a way of easing yourself into the session.

When beginning to study for the first time, you might find it useful to practise studying for short periods until you adapt and develop a rhythm.

Concentration

Stop daydreaming the moment it starts. The first law of success is concentration, and this involves learning how to cope with distractions. Eliminate irrelevant thoughts, daydreams, emotions and negative feelings. Psyche yourself up to the study task at hand by saying to yourself, 'come on, now stop wasting time and get down to business'. This little technique will help you to talk yourself back into concentration. Also, before actually studying, picture yourself effectively studying. This positive mental imagery helps create the right study mood and focuses your attention on the study task.

If you can identify a cycle of moods that you go through each week, assign the subjects you find most difficult (or like least) to the hours or day when you feel best.

Knowing you have an examination in the morning helps to concentrate the mind, so imagine you are going to be examined on the content of the study session the following day. Alternatively, imagine you will be called on to give a lecture on the topic to a group of important business people. It is well known that the best way to learn a subject is to teach it.

The study environment

The place where you decide to study should be free from all noise and distractions. However, having said that, there are some people who can study in noisy conditions. They mentally shut out the distractions. Nevertheless, noise does cause stress and therefore can never create the ideal study situation. Other people maintain that quiet background music aids rather than hinders their concentration.

You should try to study in the same place each time. You will then mentally associate a particular place with study. In fact, research suggests that students who sit for their examinations in the room where they study do better academically than those without this facility. This would suggest that your office, as it is naturally associated in the mind with work, might be a good place to study. Of course, using the office for part of your study (assuming your employer has no objections) has some advantages.

People with family commitments often find it very difficult to study at home because of noise and other distractions. Studying at night in the office may be a partial solution. Similarly, people living in flats or lodgings may find the office a convenient place to study.

Some organizations encourage the formation of study groups which meet on a regular basis. Members learn from each other by comparing notes, discussing difficult points, and setting targets for group study sessions.

Team-working is now accepted as a powerful way of learning. People bring different perspectives, abilities, knowledge and experience to the team so that everybody gains by sharing. Also, the competition inherent between individuals may also motivate the less able people in the group to work a little harder.

Sit upright on a hard chair at your desk. Sitting on a sofa is not the way to study productively! The room temperature should be warm enough to make you comfortable, but cold enough to keep you alert.

Summary

Factors such as confidence, interest and motivation will determine to a large extent how successful you are in your examination.

The mnemonic PASS will help you remember some of the key concepts in this chapter. As you will remember PASS stands for:

- **P**lan your studies
- Develop **A**ttention and concentration powers
- Have a **S**et time for study and leisure
- Work to a **S**ystem – be systematic.

It is a good idea to work to a timetable. Study sessions should not be longer than one hour, including planned breaks and review periods.

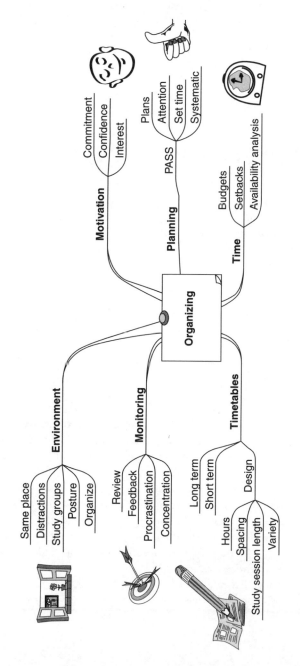

Mind Map of Chapter 2: Organizing your study

3

How to make notes

Anyone who stops learning is old, whether at twenty or eighty.
Anyone who keeps learning stays young. The greatest thing
in life is to keep your mind young.

Henry Ford

Learning objectives

- How should I take notes?
- What note-taking techniques are available?
- What are Mind Maps?
- How do I draw Mind Maps?
- What are the advantages of Mind Maps?

The value of notes

There are good reasons why you should take notes. First, they speed up the task of revision. It is a waste of valuable time if, every time you want to revise, you reread your textbooks or correspondence course material. If your notes are well made out, with key points and essential definitions for memorizing included, it is only necessary to review the notes.

Second, the preparation of notes keeps you actively involved in your studies. The actual writing activity uses your visual and kinaesthetic (i.e. sensation and muscle) functions, which aids concentration and reinforces the memory. This follows from the task of trying to ascertain key points and concepts for inclusion in your notes. Of course, the main advantage of notes is that they are a permanent record for revision, and coming up towards the examination they are essential as a timesaver.

Third, research has shown that students who take and use notes do much better in examinations than students who don't. Review your notes periodically! For good organization and flexibility, store your notes in a loose-leaf binder so that they can be classified and added to as your studies progress.

Fourth, note-taking is a good test of your listening, comprehension and short-term memory retention skills. In addition, notes can form the basis for discussion and study tasks with your fellow students.

Fifth, using notes keeps your textbook clean. Many students underline their texts or use a highlighter pen to highlight what they consider the important points. Many finish up with almost complete pages highlighted, which of course defeats the purpose of the exercise.

Note-taking techniques

There are three basic note-taking techniques available:

1. Outline notes
2. Detailed notes
3. Mind Maps.

Outline notes are compiled by listing trigger words that conjure up mental images of the key concepts and ideas in the main text. Outline notes are generally kept in conventional linear format. They may be transferred to pocket-sized cards that can be carried about and revised as the opportunity presents itself – for example, while commuting in a bus or train.

Detailed notes are the format used by most students. They are the student's version of the lecture or textbook, and may have been taken down verbatim or in summary form. If the lecture has been logically presented, the notes may stand without further revision. However, this is not often the case, and so the notes may require editing and reorganization. Frequently they need additions, involving further reading, research and reflection.

Because of its shape, the pattern form of note-taking is sometimes called a spider's web diagram. Another term is a Mind Map. Mind Maps are explored in detail later in this chapter.

Writing the notes

When reading a textbook or correspondence college course notes, don't start reading at page one and continue until the study session ends. Use the **SQ3R** method, which is a mnemonic for **S**urvey, **Q**uestion, **R**ead, **R**ecall and **R**eview. We will deal with this method in detail in Chapter 4. It is sufficient to say here that notes should not be taken until the Recall step.

If you are attending lectures as well as doing a correspondence course, you should write up your notes and review them as soon as possible after the lecture. Also, read up background material beforehand to make the lecture and note-taking more meaningful. Lecturers often fall into the trap of assuming that their audience has the same level of knowledge they have themselves.

Study textbook layouts

Most textbooks are divided into chapters. The chapters in turn are divided into sections, the sections into subsections, and these into paragraphs. For note-taking purposes, it is important to highlight the main ideas and definitions for memorization. This is not as difficult a task as it seems. Most modern textbooks are well signposted and paragraphed.

The overall concept in a chapter (or correspondence college lecture) is contained in the title of the chapter. The main ideas of the chapter are in the titles of the sections, and important supporting points are in the titles of the subsections. Significant details are somewhere in the paragraphs. This is the part where you must use your head. However, there are some tips.

The main idea of each paragraph should be in the first or last sentence. The first sentence is the topic sentence, which is usually used to introduce the main point, while the last sentence either quickly summarizes the content of the paragraph or introduces the point in the next paragraph. Watch out also for *verbal and visual signposts*, which will help you pick out important points.

When compiling your notes, use your own words. Progressive educationalists now recommend an outline form of note-taking called Mind Maps. These may be used, depending on individual taste, in preference to the more conventional methods of linear note-taking. An example of a Mind Map is given at the end of each chapter of this book.

Mind Map definition

A Mind Map is a non-linear, spatial, graphical technique where the subject matter is crystallized in a central image. The main ideas of the subject radiate from the central image as branches. Branches comprise a key image or key word printed on an associated line. Topics of lesser importance are also represented as branches attached to higher-level branches, so the branches form a connected nodal structure.

Mind Maps may be enhanced and enriched with colour, pictures, codes, symbols and dimension to add interest. These enhancements aid memory, comprehension, motivation and the recall of information.

For example, in note-taking a Mind Map may be a visual presentation and outline of the key words of a chapter, for example, in one of the student's recommended texts, distance learning units or modules. A series of micro-Mind Maps can be drawn for all the chapters of a text or distance learning unit. A macro-Mind Map can be drawn for the entire text or for the module of a distance-learning programme. Thus there is an outline macro-Mind Map of the entire book or module, supported by outline micro-Mind Maps of each chapter or unit.

Other visual methods of presentation

Mind Maps are just one method of diagrammatic representation of information that have been used in business and education for more than 20 years. With the advent of computer graphics, including Mind Mapping software programs, the use of such approaches is becoming more popular and accessible. Some of the diagrammatic representational systems include tables, graphs, bar charts, flow charts, organization charts, decision trees, Venn diagrams, algorithms and so on.

All these devices incorporate abbreviated verbal information within non-linear spatial layouts, often with colour. They differ from Mind Maps in that they have a specific use rather than a general use. For example, flowcharts as used by work-study practitioners or system analysts are a diagrammatic representation of a business procedure.

Using such methods, complex systems can be grasped quickly, analysed and made more efficient. Tables and graphs are very useful for displaying statistical information. Mind Maps, on the other hand, are general-purpose models that retain the advantages of verbal and graphical representation by using words, images, symbols and colour, while maintaining a great deal of flexibility.

Mind Maps and the brain

Mind Maps simulate the structure and organization of your brain. The average brain weighs about 3 lb (1.36 kg), which is about 2 per cent of the body, but takes 40 per cent to 50 per cent of the oxygen supply. It also uses 25 per cent of the calories we consume, and requires many nutrients.

The human brain has up to 30 billion brain cells with more than 2000 synapses or connections between each brain cell. This gives you some idea of your learning potential. Some psychologists, such as Tony Buzan, the inventor of Mind Maps, reckon that most people use less than 1 per cent of their brain's potential. In fact, to keep in top shape your brain requires love and affection, information, oxygen and nutrition.

The brain needs appropriate nutrition to function. Proper amounts of protein, carbohydrates, lecithin, and vitamin B1, in particular, are needed for good brain functioning – so make sure you take a good varied diet if you want your memory to function at its best.

For example, scientists have found that eating large amounts of choline, which is found abundantly in certain foods such as fish, can improve long-term memory in some people. This finding seems to support the old story that eating fish is good for your brain. The day may not be that far away when drugs will be available to improve memory function.

Researchers have also found that drinking lemonade containing glucose right after studying facilitates later recall. Apparently glucose helps with the chemical processes that register long-term memories in the brain.

How the brain is organized

Your brain is organized in two halves, and the two sides are connected by a large structure of 300 million neurons called the corpus callosum. Covering each side is a 1/8-inch (3-mm) thick intricately folded layer of nerve cells called the cortex. Because of it, we are able to plan, organize, remember, communicate, understand, appreciate and create: the higher intellectual skills. The left-hand side is the scientific or logic side, and is into words, numbers, analysis, synthesis and evaluation. The right-hand side is the artistic or creative side, and is into images, rhythm, colour and daydreaming.

Psychologists now think that although each hemisphere is dominant in certain activities, the mental skills identified are thought to be distributed throughout the cortex. Each side complements and improves the performance of the other. This integration can be encouraged and facilitated through appropriate learning experiences that require simultaneous processing from both hemispheres. Mind Maps maximize your learning effectiveness by drawing on both sides of the brain.

In Western society, because of the emphasis of our educational system, our logical brain tends to be highly developed and dominant. However, our creative brain tends to be comparatively neglected. Mind Maps will help us to rectify this unacceptable situation.

Making Mind Maps

Most people are unfamiliar with Mind Mapping. Because of this it is worth discussing the process in some detail and relating it to the underlying theories. The following rules are based on the Buzan method:

① Use an A4 sheet (or A3 sheet as needed) of blank paper. Draw the Mind Map landscape-style rather than portrait-style, as this gives you more space to work with. The advantage of using standard 'A' sizes is obvious from the point of view of availability, photocopying, filing and so on.

② Start the Mind Map in the centre of the page and radiate outwards. This is in contrast to linear notes, which start at the top left hand side of the page and work down. Draw a multi-coloured image in the centre to indicate the core and theme of the Mind Map. The Mind Map starts in the centre because this reflects the connective way that the brain thinks, allowing more space and freedom for developing ideas. Use image and colour because the old Confucian saying 'a picture speaks more than a thousand words' applies to both memory and creativity.

Psychologists have shown that images linked to words aid recall. Sketching is a most important aspect of the process because in figuring out how to draw a concept, the maker increases his or her understanding of it. Moving from verbalization of an idea to a visual representation requires thinking about that idea in a new way. It means considering elements that may not have suggested themselves before, and discovering new possibilities. Therefore, making images on Mind Maps encodes the information more strongly in memory and aids recall and comprehension.

③ Attach main themes to the central image because the brain works by association. Print words in large capital letters on top of thick lines of the same length as the words. The large capital letters and thick lines are used to emphasize the hierarchy and significance of ideas by making them more visible and thus more memorable. The linked nature of the Mind Map reflects the associative and connective nature of the brain.

Some psychologists maintain that human memory is a vast, intricately interconnected network. According to such models, it is not letters, syllables or words that are recorded, but concepts and propositions. The propositions are then related in various ways to other propositions, forming an associative network. The act of encoding an event is simply forming new links and associations in the network. Mind Maps show the links and relationships between key concepts, giving users an overview and a greater insight and understanding of the topic.

(4) Use a hayfork or fishbone technique to connect subsidiary lines to the main lines. These reflect the logic and associative nature of the brain. Psychologists have long established that people learn by associating new knowledge to existing knowledge and experience.

(5) Print single key words on the connecting lines (preferably one word per line). Each key word has its own range of many possible connections, and placing the key word alone on a line gives the brain more freedom to branch out in a connective fashion from that word. Phrases hide the individual word, and reduce the possibilities of further links and associations, creativity and clarity of memory. These radiant lines give the Mind Map its basic connective and associative structure. Traditional linear notes give little opportunity to add our own organization and association. Printing on Mind Maps takes longer, but it is worth the effort as it gives impact and photographic feedback to the user.

(6) Two-dimensional lettering can be used to make specific key words unique and outstanding. This is in line with the Von Restorff effect in psychology, which suggests that things are remembered better if they are made unusual. Making words unique and outstanding is an important feature of Mind Maps.

(7) Use colour throughout the Mind Map; this further enhances it, making it more interesting, unique and outstanding, and improving retention and recall. It has been found that fun and relaxation facilitates learning. This is one of the underlying assumptions of accelerated learning. It is easier to learn new things when you are relaxed and enjoying yourself. When you are bored, learning takes longer, you will tire faster, you will forget more quickly and you will need to revise more often. Colour stimulates thought, creativity and memory, and it appeals to the aesthetic senses. This will increase the brain's pleasure in building the Mind Map. Colour also increases interest and provides motivation to return to it for review.

(8) Psychologists maintain that colour is an important tool in visual thinking. It separates ideas, stimulates creativity and aids memory. Colour captures and directs attention. Even linear notes can benefit from colour coding; maps, cluster maps, mandalas and most expressive drawings are more effective in colour. When you want to highlight a key idea or point, highlighting that idea in yellow will make you (or your audience) perceive the point first. Yellow highlighters are ideal for the job of emphasizing key points on the Mind Map.

Ideally, use images, drawings, symbols and codes throughout the Mind Map to personalize its contents to represent main themes. Tests have shown that a sharp, interactive image can improve recall of word pairs by 300 per cent compared with single rote learning. Images improve problem solving and communication, and over time will improve a person's perceptual skills. Images together with colour make the content of the Mind Maps more memorable.

Geniuses including Einstein and da Vinci used images in their work. For example, Einstein's ideas came to him initially as pictures and images, which he subsequently translated into words and mathematical symbols. It is widely reported that he arrived at his theory of relativity while dreaming. He visualized what it would be like to travel down a sunbeam. Similarly, Kekule, a German chemist, discovered the molecular structure of benzene while dozing in front of the fire allowing the pattern of flames to inspire him.

Extrapolating from this, the inclusion of images on Mind Maps should help retention, recall and the generation of ideas. What is noticeable about the great scientific advances throughout history is the way people combined imagination and intuition with careful reasoned analysis. It was the partnership of right and left brain that made the crucial difference. Mind Maps harmonize left- and right-brain thinking, enhance creativity and crystallize ideas. Unless ideas are recorded, they are forgotten. Ideas externalized in a Mind Map can be explored, extended, enhanced and experimented with.

Segment the main themes by drawing boundary lines around each theme. This gives the Mind Map its unique brain-patterned shape. Miller, who discovered the magical 7 ± 2 rule in psychology, suggests that major segments should not number more than 9. Mind Maps chunk information into meaningful groups by a process of segmentation. In most practical situations there are seldom more than seven or eight subcentres, so the material in a Mind Map can be organized into a number of easily remembered chunks. Similarly, the number of chunks radiating from each subcentre again will usually be within the immediate memory capacity. Mind Maps can thus capitalize on the chunking principle by careful organization and grouping of words within segments to maximize learning and recall.

Use personalized codes and well-known abbreviations as appropriate (such as 'Mgt' for management and 'Ctee' for committee etc.). This saves space and speeds up processing, encoding and registration of information. Personalized codes using colours and arrows add a fourth dimension to Mind Maps. They enhance the Mind Mapper's ability to analyse, define, structure, organize and reason. Studies in psychology show that it is far easier for people to remember information if it is personalized. This would seem to support the use of personalized codes on Mind Maps to enhance memory.

To make information more memorable, invent mnemonics for key points. Use these as memory aids. Mnemonics have a long track record – Thomas Aquinas used mnemonic systems in teaching his monks. They were used by some of the kings of England and France, and by Shakespeare, Francis Bacon and Leibnitz. Children at school use them without any prompting. Although they are still not considered totally respectable by some academics, psychologists have now established that mnemonics can indeed improve recall.

How to identify the key words

Keyword notes are far easier to recall than phrases or sentences. The brain operates on the basis of key words and images rather than sentences, automatically dropping the inessentials, and we should do the same in note-taking. The advantages of key words are that:

1. The quantity of words is significantly reduced, facilitating faster review and revision
2. The recorded words, if chosen appropriately, are rich in imagery
3. The very act of extracting the key words improves concentration, understanding and the depth of processing.

Identifying the key words is an important aspect of the Mind Mapping process. The following are a few pointers which will help you to pick out the key points from a text when drawing up Mind Map outline notes.

Hierarchy of ideas

When producing the Mind Map from texts, use the hierarchy of ideas concept for choosing key words. In the case of the chapter, the title should give you the main idea. Note the section titles for the main ideas of the sections. The subsections should give you the important supporting points. In other words, follow the author's organizational structure.

Psychologists have found that students who have been shown words in hierarchies do far better in recall experiments than those who have been shown random lists – so structure and organization as done in Mind Maps aids recall. In textbooks, questions at the end of each chapter should alert you to what the author considers to be the key issues in the chapter.

Paragraphs

It is well established that the first sentence of a paragraph is usually the topic sentence, containing the main idea of the paragraph. Sometimes the key word in the topic sentence may be in italics. If so, the author has identified the main idea for you. Also, watch the last sentence of the paragraph, which may summarize quickly the key point or introduce the key point in the next paragraph.

The first paragraph of a chapter may give you a quick preview of what is to come, while the last paragraph may summarize what has gone before or what comes next. Similarly, the first chapter in a book may give an overview of what is to come, while the last chapter may review what has gone before. Of course, a summary at the end of a chapter, if provided, is the author's way of outlining the chapter's main ideas. Study this carefully for valuable cues as to the key points for your Mind Map.

Visual signposts

Visual signposts are used in a text to emphasize important points. They can be in the following formats:

*   Words in italics
*   Words underlined

- Words in bold face
- Numbering of points
- Lettering of points.

Other visual signposts can be in the form of tables, graphs, pictures, diagrams, algorithms, models and charts. Some people skip over these rather than examining them closely, which is worthwhile. These 'models' will clarify difficult concepts and aid comprehension, and can be usefully incorporated in your Mind Map. Remember, the more images on the Mind Map, the better the recall; diagrams which use the right hemisphere and words which use the left employ both sides of the brain.

Verbal signposts

Verbal signposts are used by authors to introduce important points. For example, 'first . . . secondly' means the author is about to list details; 'on the other hand . . . ' means the author is about to contradict a point; 'however . . . ' indicates a qualification; 'for instance . . . ' means the introduction of examples; 'therefore . . . ' indicates that the author is about to draw conclusions. These are useful cues to help you pick out the key words for your Mind Map.

The Pareto Principle

This is the law of the significant few and the trivial many. Information overload is caused by paying too much attention to the trivial many. In marketing, for example, this means that a small proportion of customers may account for a large proportion of the value of the business's turnover. Applied to writing, it suggests that a large proportion of words are superfluous and redundant (structure words, such as 'and', 'the', 'to', etc.) and are not needed for an understanding of key concepts. The reader's job is to identify the key words.

The Pareto Principle is one of the ideas on which Mind Maps are based. Sometimes people can't understand because they fail to see the wood for the trees. They avoid this by concentrating on key words and images. Mind Maps thus save considerable time when used afterwards as part of a review plan.

Recall words

Psychologists have long established that effective learners learn concepts and broad principles rather than cluttering their minds with detail. Thus, key words should be words that bring to mind the key concepts of the text. The more concrete they are, the more memorable. Concrete words converted to visual images are on the whole more easily remembered than abstract words for which imagery is difficult.

Nouns and adjectives are the easiest words to remember because they can be visualized. Thus recall words are usually nouns. They are words that trigger off other words and images, the hooks on which other words can be hung.

Uses of Mind Maps

You can of course use the Mind Map technique for more areas than just note-taking. For example, consider its application in the following areas.

Taking lectures

Use a spaced listening technique. Listen for two to three minutes, then write for half a minute. Repeat the process. Use key words only, and structure the Mind Map as you go along. After the lecture, restructure the Mind Map if necessary. This technique gives the listener more time to concentrate and reflect on the key issues of the lecture rather than being overwhelmed by superfluous detail.

Other than by shorthand, it is physically impossible to take down a lecture word for word as it is spoken. It is estimated by psychologists that speakers talk at the rate of about 135 words per minute, while we can only write at about 40wpm. Therefore, trying to take notes verbatim may result in us missing most of the lecture. Mind Maps are a type of shorthand, and will also help you focus on essential issues.

Giving lectures and public speaking

Why not use the Mind Map technique to prepare your talk? This will drastically cut down on your preparation time and give a natural flow to the delivery. Mind Maps enable the lecturer to maintain eye contact with the audience – a most important aspect of making effective presentations. It also provides the flexibility to stay within time.

One Mind Map sheet will substitute for many cue cards or sheets, which sometimes fall and get out of sequence at the worst possible time – causing much embarrassment and distress. Mind Maps are imprinted on the mind during their preparation, because of the concentration required to prepare them and their unique format, so that recall and review is facilitated.

Psychologist and author Michael J. Gelb has written an entire book, *Present Yourself* (1988), on the topic of public speaking based on the Mind Map approach. In fact, he uses a series of Mind Maps to summarize the content of the chapters in his book.

Mind Maps may also be given out to students as advance organizers. Initially students may be confused by the unconventional layout, but after a familiarization process their response to Mind Maps is almost universally favourable. Students use them as skeletal overviews to add to and customize, if they wish, while listening to the lecture. They also use them for revision and review purposes. The more personalized students make their Mind Maps, the more effective they are as learning instruments.

Writing and reports

Use the Mind Map technique for creating ideas and planning out your report. This will improve the clarity, conciseness, coherence, organization, logic and sequencing of the content of your report. In a business context, Mind Maps can banish writer's block from letters, reports and memos.

For report writing, use the Mind Map technique for planning and creating ideas. Key points can be used as headings while the supporting points can be used as subheadings. Use Mind Maps for review purposes when reading complex reports and for getting a quick overview of the key issues. Mind Maps encourage creativity, gradually building up an outline as the ideas emerge.

Similarly, Mind Maps can be used to plan books, articles, essays, assignments and dissertations. Mind Maps are a useful way of condensing, integrating, digesting and overviewing information from many sources, including research, experience, observation and reflection. Mind Maps help structure assignments in a systematic, holistic and logical fashion. Much time can be saved using this approach.

Minutes

What better way to summarize quickly the proceedings of a meeting than by the use of key words in a Mind Map! On a single page you can represent all the dynamics of a meeting and grasp its essence without reviewing pages of notes. The Mind Map can then be used to draw up the formal minutes. Mind Maps can be used to streamline meetings. Mind Maps improve note-taking, increase idea generation, facilitate group problem-solving and simplify communication. They increase productivity and save time.

Creativity and brainstorming

Why not use the Mind Map technique for creativity, problem-solving and analysis? It can be used individually or for teamwork. In business, Mind Maps have been used in such areas as marketing, manufacturing, research and development, finance, strategic planning, and training and development.

Study

Students find Mind Maps very useful as a study technique in the areas of note-taking, recall and revision. They are also a useful planning aid for essays, assignments and dissertations, and for answering exam questions.

Mind Map advantages

The linear method of note-taking presents many problems, including deciding in what order to list facts. Where will you start? When will you end? You will have problems inserting additions and making deletions as needed. However, the biggest disadvantage of conventional presentation is that it presents a homogeneous field which is difficult to learn and get motivated about, and to organize in a meaningful way. A Mind Map is a framework; organizing ideas, and its advantages can be recalled by the mnemonic 'FRAMEWORK' as follows.

Flexible

Mind Maps can be developed with new and additional pieces of information by adding them to the appropriate branch. With linear notes this creates organizational problems. Additions to Mind Maps may arise through serious and pastime reading, watching television, listening to radio, observation, discussion, experience, and critical and reflective thought. These additions may be cross-referenced to their original sources. The resultant Mind Map is a comprehensive, concentrated, conceptualized, integrated, visual and easily digestible overview and key word summary of a topic.

Psychologists have found that the major circuitry of the brain is laid down by birth, but the details and fine-tuning continue to develop throughout life. Indeed, experience itself can cause new synapses to grow. Knowledge and experiences, then, can shape the brain. Let the Mind Map be a physical manifestation of your increased knowledge and brainpower!

Recall, review and revise

Rereading of textbooks, study manuals and distance-learning modules is kept to a minimum. This gives you more time for revision of the subjects or areas that you find most difficult. Mind Maps save time, and in preparing for professional and university degrees – especially those done on a part-time basis while holding down a full-time job, often with family commitments – time management is critical to success.

Psychologists have shown that recall and review are essential to consolidate information in long-term memory and to optimize study effectiveness. A Mind Map with its key words, particularly if these are converted into mnemonics, is much easier to learn than 20 pages of linear notes. Also, the various mnemonics should be linked to each other or associated with existing stores of knowledge. Systematic review of Mind Maps will imprint the contents into your long-term memory.

Associations

Knowledge is in fact a pattern of connected ideas. It is the association of new information to existing stores of knowledge and experience that makes new knowledge meaningful. Therefore, Mind Maps will help to improve your memory. Meaningful learning happens when a person explicitly ties new knowledge to previously learnt relevant concepts or propositions. Relationships among concepts are more accessible in a two-dimensional display than in text.

Knowing how ideas are related is important for memorization. The node-link relationship in Mind Maps helps the learner to assimilate new facts and perceive how detailed information links to the central concept. Therefore, Mind Maps by their unique brain patterned spatial structure will help you to recall trigger words and their many associations, while linking the words to each other and to the central concept.

Multi-dimensional brain

Mind Maps are analogous to the brain's own system of making connections and interconnections. Mind Maps, through an interconnective model of words and images, help people integrate both sides of their brain and contribute to whole-brain learning.

Essence

The overall concept or essence highlighted at the centre of the Mind Map, with the hierarchy of ideas leading from it, provides a very clear overview. Some students fail examinations not because of insufficient work and preparation, but because they clutter up their minds with detail and are thus unable to see the wood for the trees – a type of 'paralysis by analysis'. Effective study means working smarter rather than harder. It means learning concepts and broad principles rather than cluttering up the mind with details.

Summarizing the key points in a presentation is critical to effective learning. This final step helps students see the big picture. It helps them determine whether the pieces of information they selected were the critical pieces as they begin to read the text. In memorizing anything it is vital to get an overview so that you understand the broad principles involved before you begin.

A Mind Map is an overview of the key points of a text, and thus aids memorization and comprehension. When information is simply listed, it is difficult to prioritize ideas. It is also hard to see relationships, connect ideas and see the 'big picture', and the result is a lot of information with no form of significance. The Mind Map structure graphically connects all ideas and shows the significance of each in relation to each other and to the centre.

Worthwhile visual aid

A picture is worth more than a thousand words. A Mind Map is a visual aid with impact, originality and creativity. The effectiveness of our learning is increased the more of the senses we bring into play, and the visual senses are particularly important.

Psychologists have shown that images linked to words improve recall – hence the significance of images linked to words in Mind Maps. Why not practise mentally walking the Mind Map? With training and practice, most people can improve their capacity to use images. Visualizing Mind Maps in your mind's eye will provide the training and practice and thus increase your skill at creating mental images.

Organized

Mind Maps are a structured and systematic way of getting down information and facts, just as road maps differentiate major roads (key concepts), minor roads (important ideas) and bye-ways (important detail) by the thickness of lines, codes, dimensions, colours and so on.

Psychologists have established that organization is one of the key components of a good memory. Structure influences how incoming text information is organized. Text content for which readers have a structure is said to be better organized, elaborated and remembered. For instance, researchers have shown that readers knowledgeable about soccer can recall a narrative about a fictitious soccer game better than readers who have no knowledge about soccer. Thus background knowledge helps learning of new material, and advance organizers and structure provide the key concepts that facilitate learning and retention.

Context provides a way of organizing information beforehand, thereby making it more memorable. Mind Maps provide the structure, organization and context to learn. They link new information to existing stores of knowledge in a structured framework facilitating comprehension, learning and memory.

Reconnaissance

Mind Maps will help you carry out a reconnaissance by mapping out unfamiliar terrain, particularly when used to preview chapters and complete books. Similarly, good drivers plan out unfamiliar routes by advance study of road maps. The mapping activity which Mind Maps entail imprints the information on the student's brain, making it part of the learner's own experience and knowledge.

Knowledge of left and right brain

As already stated, the brain is divided into two halves. The left side (or scientific brain) deals with language, numbers, logic and analysis, while the right side (or creative brain) deals with images, rhythm, colour and daydreaming. Mind Maps are an effective means of integrating both hemispheres.

There is increasing evidence that the ability to put thoughts into images as well as words enhances thinking skill and actually improves intelligence. Therefore the benefits of Mind Maps extend far beyond the practical application of recording ideas to higher order thinking and increased intelligence.

Summary

The main argument for note-taking in this context is that the students who take notes do better in examinations than those who do not. Notes should be categorized and filed neatly for reference in a loose-leaf binder.

The SQ3R method facilitates good note-taking. It is best to do the notes at the recall step. Mind Maps are recommended in preference to the more conventional method of linear note-taking. The rules of Mind Mapping are:

- Use an A4 sheet of blank paper
- Start the Mind Map in the centre of the page and radiate outwards
- Attach main themes to the central image
- Use a hayfork or fishbone technique to connect subsidiary lines to the main lines
- Print single key words on the connecting lines
- Use colour throughout the Mind Map
- Ideally, use images, drawings, symbols and codes throughout the Mind Map
- Segment the main themes by drawing boundary lines around each theme
- Use personalized codes and well-known abbreviations
- Invent mnemonics for key points for better recall.

In addition to study, Mind Maps can be used for a wide variety of purposes including public speaking, report writing, creativity, brainstorming and problem-solving.

The advantages of Mind Maps can be recalled by the mnemonic FRAMEWORK:

- **F**lexible
- **R**ecall
- **A**ssociations
- **M**ulti-dimensional brain
- **E**ssence
- **W**orthwhile visual aid
- **O**rganized
- **R**econnaissance
- **K**nowledge of brain.

Be creative – using images on Mind Maps encodes the information more strongly in memory.

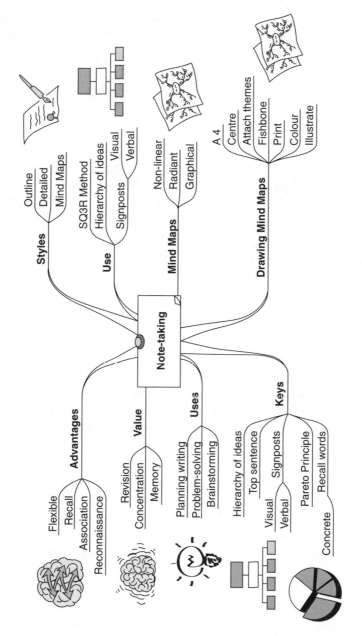

Mind Map of Chapter 3: Note-taking

4

How to tackle a textbook

Nothing in life is to be feared. It is only to be understood.
Marie Curie

Learning objectives

- What is the SQ3R method?
- How can it be used to improve my study skills?
- How can I review for exams?

Introduction – the SQ3R system

The mnemonic SQ3R stands for **S**urvey, **Q**uestion, **R**ead, **R**ecall and **R**eview. This method has been used successfully over the years in progressive colleges. It is a systematic method of tackling textbooks and correspondence course material. It is solidly based on psychological research and the methods of successful students. Let's now have a look at each of the SQ3R stages.

Survey

The survey stage, which takes five to ten minutes, is initially applied to the total book. Later you will apply the same approach to each chapter and section. This stage can be conveniently separated into three parts, namely overview, preview and inview. Survey is in fact a reconnaissance of the unfamiliar terrain in the book to enable you to build up reference points.

Overview

The first part of the survey stage is the overview, where you get familiar with the plan of the book. Look at the title page and cover. This should give an idea of the general subject matter, the level or person aimed at, the date of publication, and the author's name, background and qualifications. Has it been written with a particular examination in mind?

The next stage is to study the preface, foreword and/or introduction. This will tell you why the author wrote the book and who its target reader is. It will also give you the scope and purpose of the book, its outline and structure and how to use it.

Now turn to the contents list for an overview of the topics dealt with. It will also familiarize you with the author's plan, organization and layout. After this, study the index at the back of the book. Skim down through the entries. Is there anything familiar, or that you are already expert in? Look up the relevant section and see how the author has dealt with it. Compare this with what you know about the topic. By this technique you can judge the author's competence and knowledge of the subject and the suitability of the book for you.

Decide whether it is necessary to read the whole book or only the parts relevant to your examination syllabus. You'll have time enough to read the whole book, if you're still interested, after passing your examinations. This completes the overview stage.

Preview

Preview the actual contents. Skim through the book. Read the chapter and section headings. Study with particular care any charts, diagrams, tables, pictures and graphs. The author has included these because they illustrate some important concept where words alone would be inadequate.

Bear in mind that the ability to illustrate points made in an examination answer by including diagrams, drawings or graphs wins valuable marks; for the same reason, they are a substitute for word spinning. Glance at the occasional sentences. This is the end of the preview stage.

Inview

Now apply the same approach that you applied to the book as a whole, but this time to each chapter. Carry out a detailed survey of each chapter. Study the chapter heading, section headings, subsection headings, and the first and last sentence of each paragraph.

Write down the two or three key concepts covered in each paragraph, but watch the relative size of headings or classification system used for clues as to the importance of ideas, organization and structure. This completes the inview stage.

Question

This is the famous questioning technique familiar to organization and methods or research people. This is: What? Why? When? How? Where? Who? This puts you in a critical frame of mind. The following little verse by Rudyard Kipling will help you remember this questioning technique:

I keep six honest serving men

They taught me all I knew

Their names are What and Why and When

and How and Where and Who.

Write down your knowledge of the subject in the form of a Mind Map. Add areas to be explored, representing gaps in your knowledge and questions to be answered. Make up your own questions from headings and subheadings. Actively read in search of the answers.

Many textbooks have questions at the end of each chapter, and before tackling the chapter it is a good idea to look at these questions. Study the chapter with a view to answering these. The questions are in fact the author's method of highlighting important points essential to the proper understanding of the subject.

Read

Always read with a purpose. Actively seek answers to questions you have already constructed, and you are likely to learn. Look for the main idea of the book, chapter, section and paragraph. This is called the hierarchy of ideas, and is at four levels: level one is the book itself, level two the chapters, level three the sections and level four the paragraphs. The Survey stage is always concerned with levels one, two and three. The Read stage is concerned with in-depth study at level four.

At the first reading, don't take notes. Don't underline – this destroys a textbook. The best plan is to mark important sentences vertically along the margin lightly in pencil.

If you come to a stumbling block, skip over it after marking it with a question mark. It may not be essential to the understanding of the rest of the chapter. In any event, the material further on may better explain the problem causing the stumbling block. Then go back over it and you may find that you thoroughly understand it. The worst thing you can do when you come to a stumbling block is get discouraged and give up.

The learning curve suggests that in any learning situation you will have periods of rapid progress, slow progress and no progress. Periods of slow progress and no progress are called learning plateaus. Thus there is nothing unique or unusual about your situation; it happens to all learners.

Pay particular attention to examples, as these are used to clarify abstract concepts and make them concrete and relevant. If you still don't understand the point causing the learning block, write to your correspondence school tutor or discuss it with your lecturer, fellow students or work colleagues.

Read it again for the second time. Confirm in your own mind that you really have the main ideas at each of the levels. Pay more attention to the important details at this stage. Mark on the margin lightly in pencil the important details which should eventually be put on your mind map.

Recall

This brings you to the recall stage. Now you should take notes by recalling what you have studied and making Mind Maps. Recall by asking yourself questions and then answering them in your own words. Complete your Mind Maps by reference to the text. Advantages of recall include the following:

- Recall gives you an opportunity to discover what gaps there are in your knowledge, requiring remedial action. This is the learning principle of knowledge of results.
- Recall is an active method of study rather than a passive one. By summarizing your knowledge, you are actively involved and getting to grips with the subject.

How often should you recall? Mentally recall the main ideas involved at the end of each section. Recall at the end of each paragraph would disrupt the flow and continuity in reading. How much time should you spend in recalling? Approximately half your time should be spent in recalling what you've read.

Make your notes. Use a Mind Map to record the main ideas recalled (see Chapter 2). Complete the Mind Map from the text. Reserve a column for definitions and formulae. For definitions, rules etc., recitation is the best method of memorization.

Remember that recall, recitation combined with visualization, and paraphrasing (mentally and in writing) resembles the activity in the examination room, where you are required to recall large areas of knowledge without the aid of notes and textbooks. You are in fact judged to a significant extent by the amount you can recall.

In an examination, you get no marks unless you can actually write out the required answer in the set time. It is a test of recall, comprehension, problem-solving and time management.

Review

Unless you review, you forget 50 per cent of what you read immediately, and 80 per cent within 24 hours. Within a week 90 per cent will be forgotten, and eventually almost everything. Maintain and improve your powers of concentration by adhering to a systematic review plan. Frequent review ensures that the material in your short-term memory (STM) is transferred to your long-term memory (LTM).

Have your Mind Maps completed for the review stage. Four or five readings of textbook material may be required before its contents are familiar. If you use the Mind Maps for review, these re-readings are not required. However, you should have Mind Maps cross-referenced to the text, as this will enable you to look up relevant points in the text when you wish to do so.

Review from the Mind Maps immediately after study, within 24 hours, after 1 week, and again after 1 month. Review again after 3 months, and frequently coming up towards the examination. The theory behind this is that after the third or fourth review, the material under study goes into your LTM. Once this happens you need not review as frequently. Another advantage of review is that the ideas fit together more coherently, and there is thus less danger of having an erroneous concept in LTM.

Review plan for examinations

In addition to using your Mind Maps for review, it is a good idea to write down key ideas, difficult points or definitions on cards. Carry them around with you in your pocket for consultation during spare moments – on a bus or train for example. Review key concepts until you understand them well enough to explain them to someone else.

Some textbooks and correspondence course material have likely examination questions at the end of each chapter. These questions cover the more important points, and need particular attention.

Get past examination questions with suggested answers from the examining body. Practise answering the questions under examination conditions. Compare your attempts with the suggested answers. Make sure that if given the opportunity again you would get 100 per cent of the marks. Some examination topics come up time and time again.

Submit the relevant tests to your tutor or correspondence college on the due date. When you get them back, study the examiner's comments. This is important feedback. Learn from your mistakes and ensure that you won't repeat them again.

Finally, get past-examiners' reports from your examining body. These give you important tips regarding pitfalls to be avoided and weaknesses generally experienced by students.

Summary

The SQ3R method is recommended as a systematic approach to studying most written material. You may remember that SQ3R stands for:

- *Survey.* This in turn was further subdivided into overview, preview and inview stages. Study the preface, contents list, index, layout, chapter summaries and so on.
- *Question.* Pose questions to yourself that you want answered. Such questions may be prompted by studying the questions, if any, at the end of the chapter.
- *Read.* Read with a purpose, actively in search of answers and ideas.
- *Recall.* Try to recall the gist of what you have read at the end of each section and take notes at this stage, preferably in the form of Mind Maps.
- *Review.* Use your Mind Maps to review and revise what you have learned.

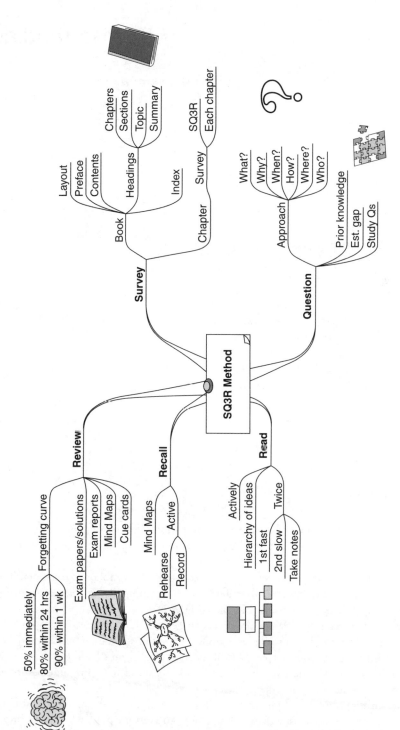

Mind Map of Chapter 4: SQ3R method

5

Effective reading

Reading is to the mind what exercise is to the body.
Sir Richard Steele

Learning objectives

- What are the barriers to effective reading?
- How are visual and verbal signposts used to emphasize important points?
- How can I improve my concentration?
- How can I improve my reading skills?
- What are the goal-focused approaches to reading?

Better reading

Before you can become a more effective reader, you should know some of the barriers to meaningful reading. A lack of understanding of written matter may not be your fault. It may be because of the author's poor presentation.

When buying textbooks, make sure they meet some of the following criteria. They should be well laid out with clear signposting, free from ambiguity, indexed, easy to read and understand, cover the syllabus, and include a glossary.

You may need to refer to different textbooks to get different perspectives. Some textbooks are better illustrated, with student-friendly explanations and clear, well thought-out examples of difficult to grasp concepts. Most important of all, you should feel comfortable with your textbook. In practice, you may have to look around for some time before you find a book that meets your particular needs.

For better reading, use the SQ3R method. This technique will help you to anticipate information and discriminate as to what is important to your purpose, what is less important and what is irrelevant.

Apply the questioning approach

When reading, adopt a 'doubting Thomas' approach. Evaluate the text in a critical and questioning way. Keep the following questions in the forefront of your mind:

1. Are the facts correct? In most reputable textbooks they probably are.
2. Does the author distinguish between facts, assumptions and opinions?
3. Are conclusions developed logically from the facts?
4. What other conclusions could be drawn?
5. Do you agree with the conclusions reached?
6. Are there contrary viewpoints?
7. Are some of the claims made unproved, or can they be supported by empirical research?

This questioning technique will make your reading more active and purposeful, with a greater understanding and retention of the material read. Watch out for limitations, exceptions, contradictions, arguments against any statement made, similarities and differences between theories discussed.

Relate the text to your own experience and more generally to your working environment. In most companies you have departments dealing with the areas you will meet in your studies – e.g. accountancy, auditing, management services, information technology, finance, marketing, law, personnel, office administration, management accounting, and purchasing and supply. Find out what is happening in these areas in your firm and relate them to your studies. You will soon begin to realize that your theoretical studies have a down-to-earth practical application.

Faster reading

It has now been established that with training, you can read considerably faster without any loss of comprehension. The average reader reads at a speed of 240 words per minute. This can be improved, with a little training, to a speed of 360 wpm. With sustained effort and plenty of practice, you can achieve 600 wpm when reading easy material.

For more difficult material, and in order to maintain comprehension levels, you should be satisfied with a reading rate of 400 wpm. On the other hand, according to research studies, there appears to be a minimal reading speed of 200 wpm below which the reader may fail to process and understand the meaning of text effectively.

Reading at a rate below 200 wpm apparently reflects inefficient, word-by-word reading which is not conducive to integrating and comprehending text in a meaningful way. Research has also shown that, when the term 'reading' is interpreted in the sense of comprehending most of the words on a page, it is impossible to read faster than 800–1000 wpm, and that comprehension suffers significantly above a speed of 400 wpm.

The capacity of the working memory is also a constraint. Of course, higher speeds can be achieved when approaches such as skimming, scanning and skipping are employed, but this should be distinguished from genuine reading.

Research has shown that the eyes move with a jerky, intermittent motion and the brain reads words at each fixation. This means you can read only when your eyes momentarily stop; each stop is called a fixation. To be a faster reader, therefore, you must increase your recognition span. The recognition or perceptual span is about three words. Reading for ideas by chunking words means that you will have fewer fixations, taking in larger groups of words with a faster reading speed.

Slow readers

In general, it has been found that ineffective readers suffer from the following:

1. They have small recognition spans, reading each word individually. This makes the flow of their reading disjointed and hinders comprehension. Try to read a whole phrase instantaneously.
2. They make regressions – their eyes drift back to reread words and phrases. This shows a lack of confidence in their reading ability, as more than likely they have absorbed what they have read. This habit destroys concentration. Making regressions may also be caused by your eyes losing their place on the page.
3. They vocalize. This is a hangover from schooldays, and as a result the speed and quality of reading suffer. However, in certain circumstances, such as revision, vocalizing can aid memory. Most readers subvocalize – i.e. say words internally to themselves. You can speed up your reading by not subvocalizing structure words, such as 'and', 'the' etc. However, subvocalizing key words has been proved by psychologists to aid memory.
4. Because ineffective readers have small recognition spans they make many eye fixations, which in turn slows down reading.
5. They do not vary their reading speed in line with their purpose, level of knowledge and the difficulty of the reading matter. Good readers see more in less time, and vary their reading rate in line with their purpose and the difficulty of the text.
6. They fail to integrate prior knowledge and experience with text information and do not apply critical reading skills, such as analysis, synthesis and evaluation, to the written text.
7. They may have a small working memory capacity and consequently less capacity for maintaining previous information and integrating new information. On the other hand, good readers with a large working memory should be able to retain more of a text in working memory while processing new text, so their integration of the information may be more thorough.

Reading techniques

Use to your benefit the difference between rapid reading, skipping, skimming, scanning and reading slowly. Skimming is where your eyes cover certain preselected sections of the text to gain a general overview. Scanning is where your eyes glance over material to find a particular piece of information.

You could employ rapid or fast reading to advantage when dealing with a novel or a not too difficult text. Obviously, with light material you can follow the storyline without reading every word carefully. If you are reading for specific information, as in research, you should skip reading matter not essential to your purpose. The index can be used to advantage here.

To survey a book, employ the skimming technique described earlier. When reading a book, get 80 per cent of the information in 20 per cent of the time by simply reading the title, headings, subheadings, last paragraph and first paragraph of each chapter. If there is a summary at the end of each chapter, you may just concentrate on these. Then reflect on the relevance of the information for you to see if you need to read in more depth.

Finally, with difficult texts you must read slowly for comprehension. The latter is the type of reading normally suitable for studying. But remember, vary your style of reading in line with the purpose. Skip or read quickly material that you are already familiar with. Read slowly material that is new to you or that you find difficult.

Seven ways to improve reading skills

Ways to improve reading skills can be brought to mind by the mnemonic 'VERTIGO', as follows.

Vocabulary

Being unable to recognize the meaning of words will slow you up considerably, although context and inference can provide clues as to meaning. You can read better if you know more words, so build up your vocabulary. To do this, you must:

1. Read widely. The greater the knowledge you already have, the easier it is to acquire more.
2. Study common prefixes and suffixes. A prefix is one or more syllables added at the beginning of a word to qualify its meaning. On the other hand, a suffix is added at the end. For example, in the word 'premeditated' the 'pre' (which means 'before') is the prefix, meditate means to think, and the 'ed' is the suffix (which refers to the past tense). Word analysis, or breaking a word into its component parts, as above, is a useful strategy to adopt for understanding words without referring to a dictionary.
3. Watch out for new words and record these on cue cards for reference. File these alphabetically and review periodically. Alternatively, carry them with you and review during spare moments of the day. As you commit the words to long-term memory, destroy the cards.
4. Use the new words you learn at every available opportunity. Integrate them into your normal everyday conversation, and thereby commit them to long-term memory.
5. Compile a glossary of technical terms in your subject or, better still, get one of the specialist dictionaries in your chosen field, if available. Use this approach to build up your technical vocabulary in your specialist subjects.

Eyesight

If your eyesight is bad and is affecting your ability to read, then get a pair of spectacles. Amazingly, many people neglect this because of vanity or inertia. During reading sessions, take a rest occasionally and focus your eyes on a distant object. This will relax and rest the eyes, and prevent fatigue.

Regression

The habit of regression is one of the main reasons why people read slowly. Stop regressing. Don't go back over words you think you don't understand – more often than not the meaning will become clear because of context and structure as you continue reading.

Talking

If you find yourself vocalizing, stop talking to yourself! However, there is one exception to this. When revising, it is often a good idea to speak the key material aloud for better impact and retention. Reduce the amount of subvocalizing and speed up your reading by avoiding subvocalizing structure words. In fact, the faster you read, the less subvocalizing you will be capable of doing.

Ideas

Read in thought (idea or concept) units. Increase your recognition span. For example, when next reading the newspaper, fix your eyes on the centre of each sentence of a column. With practice your eyes should be able to take in the beginning and end of the sentence automatically. The columnar structure of newspapers facilitates this process.

When reading a text, chunk words in groups of two or three at a time, which is the size of the perceptual span. Good readers attend primarily to the meaning of the text, while poor readers attend more to its surface characteristics.

Guide

Use a visual guide, such as your index finger, a pencil or pen. Run it along under the line you are reading without touching the page. Vary your speed in line with your purpose and the difficulty of the text as you go along. This technique focuses your attention on what you are doing and thereby improves your concentration. You won't regress through losing your place on the page.

Using your hand as a pacer allows you to see and read groups of words at a time and helps to reduce subvocalization. It adds rhythm to reading, which involves the right side of the brain. Also, two senses are involved – sight and touch – thus increasing your command.

Readers may also lose time through slow recovery time. This is the time it takes to move from one line to the next. Consciously speed up your index finger when going from one line to the next to minimize the recovery time and speed up your reading. Obviously using a guide is only appropriate for serious reading rather than leisure reading, where the emphasis is on relaxation and enjoyment.

Always maintain an upright but relaxed posture. The desk you are reading at should be of a suitable height. Some experts maintain that the distance between your eyes and the book should be between 15 and 24 inches (36 and 58 cm).

Peripheral vision is what you see out of the corner of your eyes when you are looking at something else. Experienced drivers exercise this skill every day. Without moving your eyes, you notice that a child is about to step off the footpath and run across the road. At the same time, you are concentrating and looking straight ahead.

Use your peripheral vision to read the words at the start and end of each line. You can do this by focusing your main vision a word or two from the left and right as you move down along the page. Your peripheral vision will pick up the words.

Operating reading speed

Determine your existing speed. If this is average or below, there is no reason why you can't improve it by between 50 per cent and 100 per cent without loss of comprehension – so practise reading faster. This should be done straightaway! The editorials in the newspaper each morning can be used for practice sessions. More importantly, apply the rapid reading technique to your study material as appropriate. Compete with yourself. Make each reading a step towards more effective reading.

It's a good approach to improving your reading skills if you work on one idea at a time. When you are satisfied that you are proficient in that aspect, then move on to the next idea. By this process you will build up your skills on a gradual but permanent basis. Also, for more effective and permanent learning distribute your practice over a period of time.

Improved concentration

Your concentration is an essential ingredient for successful reading. Without good concentration you will not retain and learn what you have read. Find a quiet place to read, free from noise, distractions and interruptions. Classical music, such as the baroque music of Bach and Handel, played in the background while reading can induce relaxation, make the mind alert and improve concentration.

The following are the key points for developing powers of good concentration.

Divide and conquer

Adopt a psychological attitude of divide and conquer. Instead of reading a book, read chapters. Instead of reading chapters, read sections and paragraphs. This chunking has the psychological effect of making the task more manageable and less daunting.

Instead of problems focus on benefits

The perceived benefits must outweigh the difficulties. What benefits will accrue to you as a result of reading the book? This will create interest and motivation to read the text.

Start and finish time

Estimate how long it should take to read the book. Have a time block for each reading session, with a start time and estimated finish time – 'That which can be done at any time, rarely gets done at all'. Apply time management techniques to your reading tasks (refer back to Chapter 2 for tips on how to do this).

Positive self-talk

Attitude is an important aspect of good concentration. We are what we think we are. If you think you can, you will; if you think you can't, you won't. You set your own psychological limits. To improve your concentration, say to yourself, 'My concentration is very focused. I am totally concentrated.' Feed this into your subconscious over a period of time so that it becomes part of your mental set.

Impaired concentration can be caused by a conflict between will and imagination. We must develop positive and constructive use of the imagination to help focus our powers of concentration. Relax and use repetition each day to imprint positive affirmations and images into your subconscious.

Ongoing recall

Spend up to 50 per cent of your time recalling. Take notes, preferably in Mind Map form, at the recall stage and use these for review. Adopt the 5R approach – Read, Recall, Review, Relax and Reflect. Generate images for key words, as visual memory lasts longer than verbal memory.

With models, diagrams and pictures, use your powers of visual imagination. Try to visualize the diagram or picture in your mind's eye. With practice you should get better at this. These exercises bring the right or imaginative side of the brain into play, and using both sides of your brain will enhance your learning effectiveness. Relax using a deep-breathing exercise or progressive muscle relation. People learn more effectively when relaxed.

Specific objectives

Read with a purpose. Specify your learning objectives at the outset, and self-test at the end of the reading session. Reading with specific objectives in mind directs attention and facilitates comprehension of relevant information.

Attend to task

Procrastination is the thief of time. Procrastination has been defined as the automatic postponement of an unpleasant task, for no good reason. So start now! Do it now! Take a point of view or perspective as you read to enhance your recall. Naturally, in your own case this will be the point of view of a person who wants to improve his or her reading skills. Ask yourself, how will the application of these ideas improve my reading skills?

Interest

Attention, interest and motivation are interlinked. Study with the intention to remember, as this will help you to pay attention and learn. To improve your attention, you must eliminate external and internal distractions.

To eliminate external distractions, create a proper work environment, read in a quiet place or with baroque background music, organize your workspace, use good lighting and sit in a comfortable chair.

To eliminate internal distractions, relax, know your biorhythms and plan your reading accordingly, verbalize and visualize what you want, set specific and realistic goals, and break your goals into manageable subgoals.

Interest creates motivation. Relate what you read to your own experience and existing knowledge. Whenever possible, choose areas in which you have a natural interest. People learn by linking and associating new knowledge to what they know already. The effective reader quickly integrates prior knowledge and experience with text information.

Reading approaches

When reading, vary your reading speed with your purpose. For example, the following types of goal reading approaches should be noted and used as appropriate.

Specific

You may read to research a topic of interest to you, or to get specific information for a particular problem or exam question you want to solve. Use the index at the back of the book to guide you in the particular section that interests you; then read this section carefully. This is an example of reading with a purpose.

Critical

Critical reading involves making inferences, assumptions, deductions, interpretations, predictions and evaluations. Critical reading is essential for study. You must learn to discriminate between what is important and what is not. Is it relevant or irrelevant? Is it supported by the argument or not? Apply the higher-level thinking skills, such as analysis, synthesis and evaluation, to the written text.

To support your critical reading approach, apply a creative reading strategy. Creative reading involves synthesis, integration, application and extension of ideas. It means making the reading your own, and getting more out of it through reflection and elaboration than is actually there.

Revision

Revision reading is done to confirm knowledge and help retain it in your long-term memory. Use the Mind Maps for this purpose, and be thoroughly familiar with all the main concepts. Skipping and skimming can be used with advantage here, especially when reading texts.

Informational

Additional reading is essential for most subjects, to give you familiarity and a broad background knowledge. Reading around your subject will give you different perspectives and a greater insight and understanding of the topic. However, do refer to your syllabus so that you concentrate on those aspects that are topical and relevant.

Browsing

Lunchtime often presents the opportunity to visit a bookshop or library to browse. Browsing can be an educational, relaxing and rewarding pastime, and can form an integral part of your effective study-time management system. Take the opportunity to browse through texts that do not seem wholly relevant to your syllabus. Practise your skipping and skimming techniques as appropriate, critically reading only those sections that are of importance to you.

Enjoyment

Of course, we all read for relaxation and enjoyment. As you know, when reading a novel it is not necessary to read every single word to get the gist of the story. Apply rapid reading techniques here, scanning, skipping and skimming as necessary.

Proofreading

Proofreading is an approach which is not obviously applicable to a student's needs. However, a variation on the theme, such as review or check reading, should be your approach on completing an answer in the examination. Check read for grammar, punctuation, misspellings, sense and neatness, and the positioning of decimal points. Is (A) always followed by (B), and have you demonstrated it? At work, the same approach can be applied to letters or reports prepared by you. In practice, this simple procedure is often overlooked.

Summary

For better reading, use the SQ3R method – **S**urvey, **Q**uestion, **R**ead, **R**ecall and **R**eview. The average person has a reading speed of 240 words per minute. Having highlighted some barriers to effective reading, it can be seen that by efficient reading methods this speed can be improved to about 360 wpm, with an upper limit of 600 wpm for conventional reading.

There are seven main ways in which you can improve your reading skills:

- *Vocabulary* – improve your vocabulary
- *Eyesight* – wear spectacles if you need them
- *Regression* – stop going back over words
- *Talking* – stop talking to yourself, and reduce subvocalizing or inner speech

- *Ideas* – read for main ideas, grasp them in thought units, and increase your recognition span
- *Guide* – use a visual guide, such as your index finger
- *Operating reading speed* – practise reading faster; use skipping and skimming techniques as appropriate.

Good concentration makes a key contribution to effective reading skills. The following are the key points for developing powers of good concentration:

- Divide and conquer
- Instead of problems focus on benefits
- Have start and finish times
- Positive self-talk
- Ongoing recall
- Specific objectives
- Attend to task
- Look for interest
- Proofread.

Reading with a purpose is an important aspect of effective reading. The following are the different approaches to reading:

- Specific
- Critical
- Revision
- Informational
- Browsing
- Enjoyment
- Proofreading.

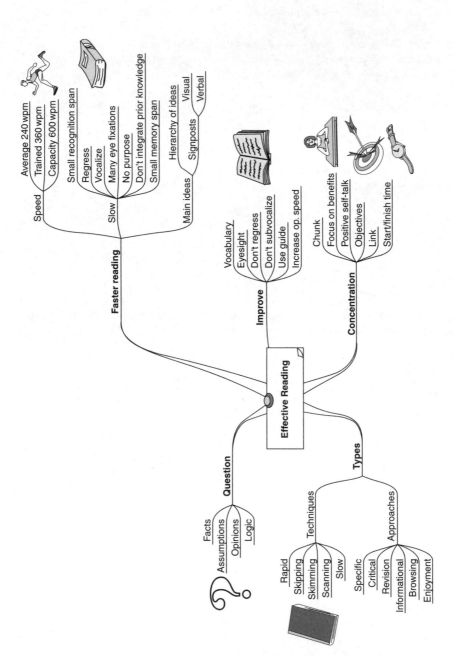

Mind Map of Chapter 5: Effective reading

6

Effective memory

A man's real possession is his memory.
In nothing else is he rich, in nothing else is he poor.

Alexander Smith.

Learning objectives

- What are the laws of remembering?
- How can I improve my memory?
- What is the PLAN system of memory?
- How can I use mnemonics to improve my recall?
- What is the systematic approach to applying memory to exam topics?

General principles

The average person uses only 10 per cent of his or her normal memory capacity. In case this 'regularly' quoted statistic is not thought-provoking enough, it is now felt that you are not using even 1 per cent of your brain's potential. There is obviously plenty of room for improvement! Memory is a very important study skill.

To pass examinations, you need to build up an adequate database of knowledge for each of the subjects on your syllabus. Most people know very little about how their memory works. Very few people get any training on memory techniques which can enhance their ability to recall information.

In this chapter I hope to give you a few practical tips that will help you remember things better, especially in the area that concerns you most – study! Throughout this chapter I will be using mnemonics as vehicles for organizing key points on memory, and also to illustrate how these devices can be used to help you recall information instantly.

A knowledge of the laws of memory and, of course, use of that knowledge can help you utilize some of the spare capacity of your brain. Let's now discuss the three laws of memory and our first mnemonic – IRA: Impression, Repetition and Association.

The three laws of memory

Impression

Get a deep, vivid impression of what you want to remember. To do this, you must concentrate and focus your attention on the material you are studying. Use your powers of observation. A camera won't take good pictures in poor lighting conditions; similarly, your mind won't register and remember impressions when there are inconsistencies in your mental ideas of a subject.

Impression is therefore the ability to imagine or picture what you want to remember in your mind's eye. Reading is a left-brain function. The left side of the brain specializes in logic, words, numbers and language. To make your reading more memorable you also need to use the right-hand side of the brain, which specializes in creativity, imagination, colour and daydreaming. So when you're reading, try to live and visualize the experience. At first you may find this difficult to do; nevertheless, the very fact that you are trying will improve your concentration and thus help you remember information better.

Use your senses

External impressions such as sight, sound, smell, touch and taste are obtained by keeping your eyes open, observing and actively getting involved in the world about you. Internal impressions such as interest, understanding and attention are obtained by closing your eyes, visualizing and reflecting on your experience. For example, when trying to recall a section of a book, you could try to visualize the key points in your mind's eye – or, better still, write them down.

Employ all your different senses – visual for pages, diagrams and pictures; auditory for paraphrasing, recitation and reading aloud; the sense of touch and imagination for note-taking and visualization. Forming mental images or drawing diagrams or flowcharts of key study material will help you to understand it.

Drawing or note-taking uses the left or verbal side of the brain, while using imagination draws on the right or visual side of your brain. Thus your ability to recall the information is more than doubled.

Visualization

Forming mental images or drawing diagrams or flowcharts about study topics will help you to understand and to imprint the information on your mind. Some educationalists argue that this is effective because it involves the left (logic) and right (creative) hemispheres of the brain. On the other hand, drawing diagrams or flowcharts brings the right or creative side of the brain into action. Thus your chances of understanding and recalling the information are multiplied.

Live the experiences by visualizing the use of as many of the senses as possible. For example, when studying company law, picture the process involved when registering a limited company. Imagine yourself completing the necessary documentation. Sense the feel of the paper. Picture the inside of Companies House, and the bureaucratic hassle you might go through to get the registration finalized. To make the process stand out in your mind even more, imagine you have a ferocious argument with the official at Companies House about some aspect of the procedure.

Discuss a lecture or chapter with a fellow student after listening to or reading it. The discussion will give you different perspectives on the topic while holding your concentration and stimulating your mind. It also brings variety to the study approach. Set up formal study sessions groups to discuss course-related topics. Set aside one or two hours, say each Saturday morning, for this purpose.

Develop an interest in your topic for better learning and recall. Read around your topic. At the very least, read an appropriate professional journal and the business pages in the newspapers. Interest creates motivation and counteracts boredom. Integrate what you want to remember into your everyday activities. Information is forgotten quickly if not actively used.

Use the MUSE principle

If you dramatize, personalize and emotionalize something, you are more likely to remember it. Therefore put **M**ovement, **U**nusualness, **S**lapstick and **E**xaggeration into your mental images:

- **M**ovement – adding movement to an image makes it more vivid, exciting and memorable
- **U**nusualness – bizarre, weird or sexual images are particularly easy to remember
- **S**lapstick – humorous situations are easier to remember than normal ones
- **E**xaggeration – exaggerate the size and number of the items for better recall.

Vivid, colourful images are easier to remember than drab ones, so remember the mnemonic MUSE (in mythology, a Muse was one of the nine goddesses inspiring learning and the arts) for more effective recall.

Study material is retained better if it answers a question. Put down in a Mind Map the amount of knowledge that you already have on the topic, and the answers to the questions that you seek. This is the knowledge gap. This exercise creates the proper mental set or attitude for study.

The three Rs of memory

The three Rs of memory are **R**eception, **R**etention and **R**ecall. GIGO is a well-known mnemonic used in computer circles, and stands for 'garbage in, garbage out'. The same idea can be used in learning and memory. Obviously, to remember something you've got to register it on your imagination. Constantly reflecting and thinking about your subject will make sure this process takes place, which ensures that the information is retained in your long-term memory. What you are doing, of course, is overlearning the information.

Recall is the ability to be able to reproduce the material in writing inside the exam room without the support of books for reference. When recalling, use your vivid imagination. Written words in themselves are dead. The author had pictures in his head before actually writing the words, and you must translate the words back into pictures.

Repetition

The second law of memory is repetition. Muslim students memorize the *Koran* – a book as long as the New Testament – by repetition. Repetition is how we learnt the times tables at school, and also the alphabet. Psychologists call this overlearning. The material has been embedded in our long-term memory. This is the approach you need to adopt when learning key points and important definitions. I would not recommend rote learning except in this particular instance. Build up your database of key points and concepts in your topic, and you can expand on these yourself. When using the repetition technique, keep the following points in mind.

Review plan

Space out your repetition for better recall. Go over it a few times, then drop it; come back later and go over it again. Reviewing at intervals in this manner will help you to memorize things in about half the time it takes to do so at one sitting.

Keep a review file. Imagine you take some notes on 1 January. Do review 1 on 1 January, and date your notes for the second review. In this case it will be on 2 January – i.e. 24 hours later. Therefore, put 2 January on the top of your notes. Review 3 will be on 9 January. Review 4 will be on 9 February. Review 5 will be on 9 June. This will anchor the key points into your long-term memory. Every day check the date on each page of your notes. Notes with today's date on them should be reviewed now and then forward dated for the next review.

In general, review from Mind Maps, cue cards, review questions at the end of chapters, past exam questions and answers, lecturer's comments and examiner's reports.

Discuss the chapter with a colleague after reading it, and thereby reinforce the memory of it. When reading, imagine that you will be called on to give a lecture on the topic. This has the marvellous effect of focusing the mind on the topic. On a lower key, imagine that you will be required to explain it to a friend after reading it.

Recall frequently

Recall at the end of each section and again at the end of each chapter. Paraphrase the author's thoughts in your own words. Recalling constantly aids reading comprehension and monitors progress. The first time you do this, write down the points you can recall. Compare these with the text and fill in the gaps, and then use these notes to compile your Mind Maps of key points. In a typical study session, spend 50 per cent of your time recalling. Continuous feedback through recall is essential for effective memory.

Think about your subject during spare moments of the day – for example, walking along the street, waiting for a bus or commuting to and from work. Use cue cards for this purpose. The famous American psychologist William James said: 'the one who thinks over his experiences most and weaves them into systematic relations with each other will be the one with the best memory'.

In recalling information, don't just verbalize the recall; write it down. Better still, do a Mind Map of the key points. This is a left-brain activity. To make it more memorable, reflect on the topic and actively associate information to make it unique and outstanding. Picture the information in your mind's eye. This process draws on the right side of your brain.

Association

The third law of memory is association. Association means linking study material with information and experience that you already have. Relate your professional studies to your work, and try to integrate them with your everyday life experience.

Apply the questioning technique to build up the necessary links and to engrave the subject matter on your memory. Why is this so? How is this so? When is it so? Where is it so? Who said it? What else could be deduced? The more the brain is used, the more memory associations are formed. The more associations are formed, the easier it is to remember previously acquired information, and also to form new associations.

The three laws of association

There are three laws of association which you may find useful to know. The first law is called the law of similarity. This states that two ideas may be associated if they resemble each other – for example, people with the same name.

The second law of association is called the law of contrast. This states that two ideas may be associated if they contrast with each other – for example, tall and short, day and night. These laws suggests that comparing and contrasting ideas is a very effective way of learning information.

The third law is called the law of contiguity. This states that two ideas may be associated if they have occurred together – for example, if two important events happened on similar or near enough dates, one may be recalled by reference to the other. We all know that the First World War started in 1914. Frederick Winslow Taylor, the 'father of scientific management', died the following year in 1915. Connect the two events, and you have a way of recalling the date of Taylor's death.

Information is retained better if it is obtained in answer to a question. This creates active learning and the proper mental set. Put down in Mind Map form the knowledge you already have about the topic and the questions that you want answered. Develop an interest in the subject, as this will improve your ability to learn and recall. Integrate what you want to remember into everyday activities. Things are forgotten through disuse.

Organize your material for better recall

People tend to have better recall of items that are linked, categorized and conceptually related in some way. Mind Maps will help you to do this. Short-term memory (STM) is the amount of information a person can recognize and recall after a single presentation without practice. STM decays rapidly without rehearsal, with estimates ranging up to 18 seconds' duration. Like long-term memory, interference seems to be the prime cause of forgetting in STM.

The capacity of STM is between 5 and 9 items of information. However, its capacity can be extended if the material is grouped. For example, a memory span of 7 letters can be increased to 35 if the letters form 7×5-letter words. Therefore, 'chunk' the learning points into related groups of between 5 and 9 items. Thus isolated words such as mnemonics can be easily memorized if you are astute enough to organize them into a meaningful sentence or a little story. Whole areas of a topic can therefore be recalled quite easily.

In memorizing, say, a definition, the central part requires more attention than the two extremes. So make the central part unique and outstanding and you will remember it better.

Use the SQ3R method described earlier. The Survey, Question part of this formula gives you the framework and hooks to associate information to as you read. Information that is organized can be learnt much faster than information which is not. Reading strategies that pay attention to individual ideas, and to how they are organized and related, produce better recall.

There are three techniques for mental organization:

1. Sequencing, which means putting items into chronological or alphabetical order.
2. Categorizing, which means grouping items according to some common characteristic such as colour, shape or other similarity.
3. Relational imagery, which means organizing items round a theme such as work, holidays, Christmas etc. People remember things better in relation to a particular context. Contextual features become associated with material being learned, and can serve as cues for recall.

Memory and understanding

Let's now look at the 'MUD' principle. MUD is a mnemonic standing for **M**emory, **U**nderstanding and **D**oing. Obviously, if you really want to remember something you should understand it. Memory is but one of the ingredients of effective learning. Memorizing involves association, repetition, review, paraphrasing and self-testing; understanding involves questioning, comparing, contrasting, analysis, synthesis and problem-solving; and doing involves a physical activity of some sort with practice sessions to achieve perfection.

Professional and university examinations test students' capacity to demonstrate their analytical and problem-solving abilities rather than mere rote memorization. Therefore, organize your material, be thorough, and make sure that you understand what you are committing to memory.

The greater our existing knowledge, the greater our insight, understanding and ability to make meaningful associations. Wide and extensive reading will provide a sound foundation on which additional knowledge can be built. Pay attention to meanings, and make extensive use of associations.

Look for similarities, contrasts, advantages and disadvantages, and relate everything you can to your fund of knowledge and experience. Use the SQ3R system for better understanding, retention and recall.

The memory model – FIBRES

Brain cells, when viewed under a microscope, look like tiny octopuses with tentacles or fibres emanating from them. This should help you link the mnemonic FIBRES with memory. FIBRES is really an elaboration of the three basic laws discussed in the previous few paragraphs. FIBRES stands for **F**requency, **I**ntensity, **B**elonging, **R**ecency, **E**ffect (Pygmalion) and **S**tand out (unique and outstanding). Let's now look at each of these laws!

Frequency

Frequency means exactly the same as repetition. The more often you learn, the better you know it. Overlearn, so that in the examination room you won't have difficulty recalling information – even if under stress.

The best way to commit a passage to memory is by the 'progressive part method'. In this method, the learner adds a new line while continuing to rehearse the other lines. For example, if you learn line one, you should then learn lines one and two. When you have these memorized, you should tackle lines one, two and three, and so on. Such a procedure ensures:

- That our short-term memory is not overloaded
- The practice and retention of earlier lines, otherwise forgotten through interference.

For best results, the 'progressive part method' should be combined with the 'holistic method' (see below). In other words, get an overview of the material first before using the progressive part method. This is the concept behind the SQ3R system. Build up a framework of the area to be studied, and then develop this as your studies progress.

Intensity

Intensity, motivation, interest and confidence are all interlinked. Each reinforces the other. The more success you have, the more confident and motivated you become. Similarly, the more enthusiastic you are about a topic, the better your recall. For example, a schoolboy may be thought to be stupid and indifferent at studies and yet have an amazing capacity to recall all the players in his favourite football team, which matches they won and even who scored the vital goals. The reason for this, of course, is that soccer has caught his imagination and interest.

In reality, it is hard to have an intense interest in all the topics that you study; nevertheless, be aware of this factor and try to build up enthusiasm and interest for these subjects. Develop intense powers of attention and concentration to memorize and study effectively.

Belonging

This is sometimes called the 'holistic method'. The mind likes to get an overview of a topic before it starts filling in the details – just as we tackle a jigsaw puzzle. We look at the illustration and then start working from the outer edges and work our way inwards. We are using a telescopic approach, going from less detail to more detail. Psychologists call this the 'gestalt' approach. Of course, Mind Maps are an application of this idea.

Recency/primacy

Recency means we remember better what we did last – that is, most recently. Primacy means we remember better what we did first rather than what came subsequently. We remember our first day at school, our first day at work, our first love affair etc. This is the novelty concept and the reason why as a child you learnt so well. Things are impressed on your memory when they are new and novel. So when studying a subject for the first time consciously make as much use of the novelty concept as possible.

The recency/primacy principle suggests the more starts and finishes there are in a study period, the better. Of course, after each study period take a five-minute break. To maintain your level of concentration, keep your study sessions to one hour's duration or less with short rests inbetween for review and consolidation of information. Immediately after you have learnt something is the time when your memory for it is best. This is called the 'reminiscence effect'. Frequent breaks allow you to take advantage of this.

Effect

This is the 'Pygmalion effect'. Educationalists have found that praise produces greater effort than criticism. Thus a little praise now and again will reinforce your motivation to succeed. By the way, don't wait around for other people to praise you; 'self-stroking' or praising yourself is a type of auto-suggestion, and is nearly as effective. This also builds up your self-esteem and powers of positive thinking. The Pygmalion effect suggests that students live up to role model expectations of them, so if you have a teacher who treats you as an intelligent, mature and able person and sets you high standards of performance you are likely to live up to those expectations.

Feelings of competition often intensify the study effort. This phenomenon is well known to training managers, who use the case study method to get participants competitively and imaginatively involved in the learning process. This suggests that it might be more productive to form study groups.

Stand out (outstanding)

In psychology this is called the Von Restorff effect. If you want to recall something, make it unique and outstanding. Remember the 'MUSE' principle? MUSE is a mnemonic standing for movement, unusualness, slapstick and exaggeration. In other words, if you want to remember something visualize it in an unusual context, using vivid imagination, colour, exaggeration and humour. This will make the information more memorable.

The PLAN system of memory

PLAN is a mnemonic which stands for the main systems of memory. These are:

- **P**lace system
- **L**ink system
- **A**lphabet system
- **N**umber rhyme and number shape.

Place system

The basic idea in the place system is to use the items of furniture in each room in your home as hooks to associate or link things to. The hooks might be door, lamp, window, clock, chair, table, plant, TV, cabinet and fireplace. Associate the items you want to remember with these links, and then when you want to remember them you take a mental walk around your house picking off the items as you go around.

It is easier to associate items with familiar pegs, which is the advantage of the room system. It is also expandable in relation to the number of rooms and items in each room in your home. The pegs can also be items you encounter on a familiar walk or car journey. For abstract items you may have to use substitute concrete words. An example of this might be Justice, Liberty and Fraternity. To remember these, just think of a judge, the Statue of Liberty, and a group of your relatives who have turned up unexpectedly. Visualize the judge sitting on your favourite fireside chair, the Statue of Liberty on top of the TV, and your relatives sitting on the sofa. Use the 'MUSE' principle to imprint the items on your memory – movement; unusualness; slapstick and exaggeration.

Link system

This uses your powers of vivid imagination to associate items together in sequence. Again, use the MUSE principle when doing so. In other words, see things in an action-related context; larger than life; millions of them; in a humorous situation and in colour. As an example, say you want to remember dog, television, pencil and apple. Just picture the dog devouring the TV, the TV with pencils stuck out of the screen, and apples being knifed with pencils. The more vivid and unusual the association, the better you'll recall it.

Alphabet system

In your early school days you committed to memory the 26 letters of the alphabet. This means that you have 26 hooks for associating things to. The idea here is to invent words to represent each letter of the alphabet and commit these to long-term memory. For example, A might be axe; B might be bee; C might be sea; D might be deed and so on. If you want to remember 26 items, you link or associate them with these ready-made hooks.

Number rhyme and number shape

The number rhyme is a well-known memory system used in scores of memory books. It goes like this: 1 is gun; 2 is shoe; 3 is tree; 4 is door; 5 is hive; 6 is sticks; 7 is heaven; 8 is gate; 9 is wine; 10 is hen. The same principle of associating items you want to remember with these easily recallable hooks is used.

Number shape

The number shape is based on the idea of animated digits. The number 1 here could be a pole; 2 a swan; 3 a butterfly; 4 a sailing boat; 5 a sickle; 6 a snake in the form of a six; 7 the bow of a ship; 8 an hourglass; 9 a walking stick; and 10 a bat and ball. These could be used as hooks, or substituted for numbers. In this way, to recall 26 you could visualize a swan devouring a snake.

You won't learn to drive a car by reading a book. Similarly, it takes considerable time, patience and practice to get proficient in the PLAN system of memory. Nevertheless, your efforts will be more than adequately rewarded by the development of an outstanding memory in your area of expertise. Nothing worthwhile is easy to learn and master, so start now, practise and persevere.

Making memory mnemonics

Mnemonics have been used throughout this book, as they are very useful when trying to jog memory. Don't overdo them, however, or you'll have a job trying to remember the mnemonics! Use them sparingly for greater effect. The rhyme 'thirty days hath September ...' helps us to remember the number of days in each month of the year. A well-known mnemonic for remembering the chemical constituents of coal is NO CASH where N stands for nitrogen, O for oxygen, C for carbon, A for ash, S for sulphur and H for hydrogen.

If you find it difficult to get the letter combinations to make up words, use an aid such as *The Word Game Winning Dictionary* by Bruce Wetterau, or other 'Scrabble' aid word books. Also, a good dictionary and a *Roget's Thesaurus* are indispensable. Use mnemonics and visual imagination to put fun back into learning, making it personalized, exciting and enjoyable, as it should be.

A mnemonist is a person with a trained memory. Why not use some of the devices these experts use? Examples of mnemonics include:

- PEST, which is used for environmental analysis and stands for Political, Economic, Social and Technological.
- PAIN, which is used for recalling the various investment appraisal methods and stands for Payback, Accounting rate of return, Internal rate of return and Net present value.
- PLOCS, which recalls the main functions of management and stands for Planning, Leading, Organizing, Controlling and Staffing.
- SREDIM, which is the work study approach to solving problems. This nonsense word stands for Select, Record, Examine, Develop, Install and Maintain. This can also be adapted and used to recall the key steps in the problem-solving or decision-making process.
- AIDA, which is an aspect of sales promotion and stands for Attention, Interest, Desire and Action.
- DAGMAR, which stands for Defining Advertising Goals for Measured Advertising Results.
- SPEWSIC, which is a nonsense word that will help you remember the strategic planning process: Strategic objectives; Position audit; Environmental analysis; WOTS UP analysis; Strategies to fill the gap; Implementation and Control.
- SMART, which may be used to help you remember the characteristics of good objectives. They should be Specific; Measurable; Attainable; Realistic and Timely.
- APES, which may help you remember the major controls in a business. This mnemonic stands for Annual plan control; Profitability control; Efficiency control and Strategic control.

To remember the names of the planets in our solar system, use the sentence 'My Very Educated Mother Just Showed Us Nine Planets'. This stands for Mercury, Venus, Earth, Mars, Jupiter, Saturn, Uranus, Neptune and Pluto. The colours of the rainbow can easily be remember by 'Richard Of York Gave Battle In Vain' – red, orange, yellow, green, blue, indigo and violet.

You have probably come across the memory device for remembering that stalactites hang on the ceiling of caves (c for ceiling, and tights down) while stalagmites come from the cave floor up (g for ground, and mites up). Principle and principal are two words which are often mis-spelt and confused; to remember them for all time learn 'principle is a rule while principal is a pal'. If you have problems remembering how to spell 'believe', just remember 'never believe a lie'. To distinguish 'stationery' from 'stationary', just visualize a large Envelope for stationery.

Why not invent your own mnemonics for critical areas of your studies or work, or for vital information that you need to remember? Research shows that when people are given only a short time to study a list, those using mnemonics learn two to three times better than those who use their usual approach.

Systematic use of memory for examinations

Memory is the receptacle and sheath of all knowledge.
Cicero

Initially, in any subject there are basic facts you must acquire before you can progress to a higher level of understanding. The following systematic approach to the learning and memorization of these facts is recommended:

1. For each subject, and from study up of to ten previous examination papers and the syllabus, identify key areas and topics which recur.
2. Identify the important definitions (about half a dozen) facts and concepts in these areas.
3. Write definitions on cards, put these in alphabetical order and take them around with you for revision during spare moments of the day.
4. Invent mnemonics for topical examination issues using key words only, and practise as in (3). For related topics link the mnemonics to form sentences, or create a little story for maximum recall.
5. Have sets of cards for each subject, and designate certain days of each week on a rotational basis for each subject area – for example, Monday (financial management), Tuesday (company law), Wednesday (management) and so on.
6. Prepare Mind Maps of mnemonics covering an integrated area of each subject, and use these to establish links between topics. This will help you develop your powers of knowledge, comprehension, application, analysis, synthesis, evaluation and problem-solving
7. Practice makes perfect. Practice makes permanent. Overlearning will make vital information part of your own thought process, enabling you to apply it to particular examination problems as necessary.

Memory and drugs

When studying, always be alert. Alertness and concentration are vital to successful studying. Alcohol and drugs, apart from destroying brain cells, also impede concentration, and should not be taken when studying. The odd cup of tea or coffee will help you keep alert. Try to stay physically fit and keep to a nutritious diet, as maintaining health is an important aspect of studying.

Video, audio cassettes, CDs and DVDs

Watch the Open University programmes on BBC television and business programmes generally for lectures and topics relevant to your syllabus. The Open University has many excellent lectures on economics, management, accountancy, finance, information technology and so on. If you have a video recorder, some of these programmes might be worth recording for review purposes.

In any event, you might be able to persuade the training officer in your company to hire or purchase some of the better lectures from the BBC or elsewhere for viewing and discussion by your study group.

There is now a wide variety of examination related topics available on cassette tapes, CDs, DVDs and CD-ROMs. Use these as appropriate for study and revision. If your company has an open learning centre, use it. There are now very good computer-based training packages on all aspects of business.

Summary

The following are the main tips and techniques for developing a good memory for examinations:

- Ongoing recall
- Pose questions
- Techniques (PLAN – place, link, alphabet, number rhyme and number shape systems)
- Interest
- Mnemonics
- Integrate your studies into your life
- STM v LTM; know the role of STM and LTM memory in recall
- Thinking/reflection
- Imagination and visualization
- Categorization and chunking.

Be optimistic about your ability to develop a good memory. Believe in yourself. If you think you can, you will. If you think you can't, you won't. Practise the memory techniques outlined in this chapter.

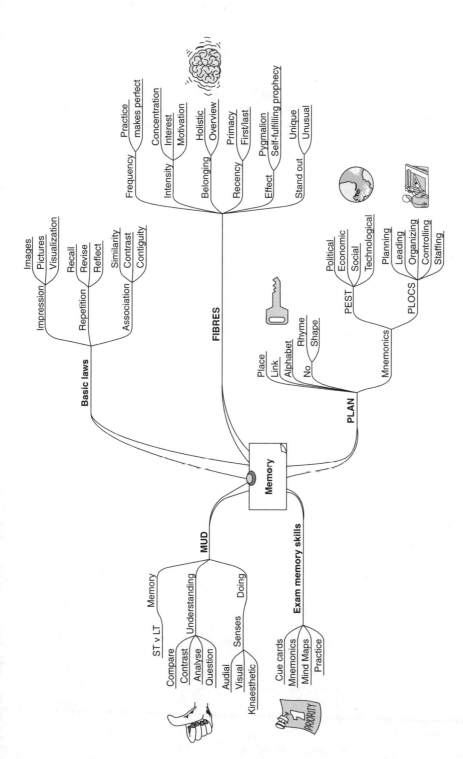

Mind Map of Chapter 6: Memory

7

Case studies

It is not enough to have a good mind. The main thing is to use it well.

René Descartes

Learning objectives

- What is the rationale behind case studies?
- What is the systematic approach to tackling case studies?
- How can I apply this to gain more marks when answering case studies?
- What are the three main faults examiners find with students in answering case studies?

Introduction

Case studies are scenarios based on actual problems experienced by organizations and that are used as vehicles for discussion, analysis and solution. They may include the history of an organization; the key management players; production information such as a production plan; financial information such as past trading, profit and loss accounts, cash flow statements and balance sheets; marketing information such as marketing plans; and details about competition. HRM policies and potential industrial relations problems may be part of the scenario. Students may be asked to devise a solution based on assumptions about resources, and economic and legal restraints, and to develop an implementation plan.

Case studies are now being used in university and professional examinations to test students' ability to apply their knowledge in a practical context. Traditional exam-type questions are good at testing a student's knowledge and the ability to communicate ideas lucidly in a limited time. On the other hand, case studies are good at assessing a student's ability to analyse complex situations, to interrelate different subjects, solve problems, make decisions and evaluate alternative courses of action.

Case studies test comprehension

Case studies can be written to incorporate the desired level of difficulty in line with the requirements of the syllabus. CIMA has a major case study in the final stages of its exams. From 2005 this case study will be called the Test of Professional Competence in Management Accounting (TOPCIMA), although it will be similar to the current case study in terms of the assessment format. The purpose of TOPCIMA is to test students' ability to demonstrate key business skills. Case studies are also an important aspect of MBA programmes, marketing programmes, human resource management programmes and other business degrees.

Case studies are designed to test students' powers of absorption, comprehension, conceptualization, application, integration, analysis, synthesis, judgement, creativity, communication and evaluation. The examiner is trying to test your ability to apply your studies to problems in a logical, analytical, practical and systematic fashion. Are you aware of the causes of the problems before selecting the possible solutions?

Information given in case studies is often incomplete, simulating the type of situation that managers are faced with daily in practice, when they have to come to decisions based on incomplete facts and under exacting time constraints. Similarly, in the examination room you will be dealing with open-ended cases with insufficient information and incomplete facts while working to a strict time deadline. To do this you must be able to integrate, adapt and apply your knowledge to the particular problem that any question describes.

You need to have:

- A flexible and creative approach
- Realistic opinions
- Practical recommendations.

For example, marketing, business management and strategic planning questions, unlike management accounting questions, do not have a correct numerical answer, and it would usually be wrong and wasteful of valuable time to look for a correct or complete answer in any figure work that you do. In a past examiners' report, the examiner wrote:

The management accountant has to know how to extrapolate from the data at hand to obtain the information needed. Where critical variables cannot be quantified he may have to point to assumptions included in his analysis or provide guidance as to its sensitivity.

Case studies are therefore open-ended, and assumptions have to be made about missing and incomplete information.

SREDIM

There is a well-known approach to solving problems which can be recalled by the mnemonic SREDIM. This approach is as follows:

- **S**elect the problem for study. Make sure that you understand what the real problem is.
- **R**ecord the facts given. Differentiate between facts, assumptions and opinions.

- **E**xamine, analyse and interpret. Adopt a critical, questioning and sceptical attitude as appropriate. Examine the purpose (What is done? Why is it done? What else might be done? What should be done?), the person (Who does it? Why does that person do it? Who else might do it? Who should do it?), the place (Where is it done? Why is it done there? Where else might it be done? Where should it be done?), the sequence (When is it done? Why is it done then? When might it be done? When should it be done?), and the means (How is it done? Why is it done that way? How else might it be done? How should it be done?).
- **D**evelop alternative solutions. Flexibility of mind and creativity is needed here. In how many different ways could this problem be solved?
- **I**mplement – choose and put into operation the best alternative.
- **M**aintain and follow up to ensure that your solution has worked out satisfactorily.

Systematic approach to case studies

First read through the case study quickly to familiarize yourself with it. Then read it in detail, applying the systematic approach to case studies as follows.

Identify the problem

Identify the problem (or problems) and issues involved. Identify the real problem. Einstein wrote:

The formulation of a problem is far more essential than its solution, which may be merely a matter of mathematical or experimental skill. To raise new questions, new possibilities, to regard old problems from a new angle, requires creative imagination.

Do not confuse the symptoms with the problem. For example, an influenza virus causes a headache, sore throat, sneezing, tiredness, perspiration and aching joints. These are symptoms; the action of a virus is the problem. However, identifying the symptoms may help you to identify the problem.

What is a problem? In very simple terms, it's the difference (the gap) between an actual situation and some desired state. In strategic management this is called gap analysis, the gap being the difference between the existing or extrapolated position and the corporate objective. The gap is filled by the implementation of appropriate strategies.

The first step is to understand the existing situation as given in the case study. In strategic planning this is called the position audit or situation analysis. The second step is to compare this with the desired state in which the organization would prefer to be. Remember that there is likely to be more than one problem facing an organization. The position audit under the 'eight Ms' (**M**anpower, **M**oney, **M**aterials, **M**achines, **M**anagement, **M**anagement structure and culture, **M**arketing and **M**anagement information systems) classification may help you to identify the major problem categories.

You should state the problems as precisely as possible. All problems will not be of equal importance, so you must prioritize your list of problems, focusing on the solution of those with the greatest pay-off.

Problems are usually interlinked, and interact and affect each other in a complex, multi-faceted manner. For example, many case studies are usually written around specific issues. The problem for solution is normally set out by the examiner in the questioning approach – what is the problem (or problems)? Where does it occur? When does it occur? Whose problem is it? Why does the problem occur? What are the reasons for the problem? How can the problem be overcome?

In business organizations, problems may be caused at corporate, functional or line levels by, among other things, poor performance or standards in planning, leadership, motivation, control, communication, co-ordination, setting objectives, time management, delegation and interpersonal relationships; interdepartmental conflicts; organizational politics; discipline; and many more. Remember that a problem well stated is halfway to being solved.

Record the facts

Record and summarize the facts given, and focus on the facts appropriate to the solution of the questions asked. The following are some of the facts that may be provided in a case study:

- *Mission statement.* This provides the reason for the existence of the business, provides the driving force and direction, and is critical to the decision-making process.
- *Corporate objectives.* These may be given, but frequently are not stated explicitly. You may have implicitly to assume from the facts given what the corporate, business and functional objectives are.
- *Management structure.* This is usually given, and you can ascertain the degree of formality and centralization. Consider whether the structure, management style and culture are suitable for the type of environment that the company is operating in.
- *Marketing.* Examine the company's marketing strategy, market share and state of competition.
- *Management information systems.* These should be adequate to support management decision-making. Too much control may be symptomatic of bureaucracy, while too little control may leave the business open to undue risk.
- *Managerial style.* Consider the knowledge, skills and expertise of the management. How does senior management interact with other management levels? Take a view on the managerial style, communications and decision-making processes.
- *Functional policies.* Address functional issues to identify the policies pursued and how they relate to the overall corporate objectives.
- *Human resource management.* Consider the HRM management in the company, particularly in relation to industrial relations and training and development.
- *Finance.* Consider the financial position of the company by examining financial statements provided. Consider profitability, return on capital employed, liquidity, gearing and any other relevant issues. Have regard to comparable companies within the industry sector.

More importantly, identify the facts that are not given but that in practice would need to be taken into account for a good decision. Why do case study writers leave out information or give incomplete information? There are three possibilities:

1. The information may have been unobtainable.
2. Information was left out deliberately because its omission made for a better and more focused case study. Logistical information may have been excluded because the case writer wishes students to concentrate on the strategic and organizational aspects of the case. Production and personnel information may be excluded because the case writer wants to focus the examinee's attention on the marketing issues. Students sometimes think that because certain information is not provided it is irrelevant. This is not a wise assumption.
3. In some examinations, case studies must be kept to a reasonable length because of the time limitation. Information, therefore, is not included because of the necessity to keep the case study short. This would suggest that only essential information is given, peripheral information being excluded. Therefore, missing information may have to be assumed or extrapolated by the student.

If faced with a similar problem in a work situation, how would you solve it? This will force you to consider the practical implications and constraints associated with the problem. Where figures are provided, they may also be incomplete.

Examiners' reports are invaluable sources of guidance on exactly what is required. For example, an examiner in management made the following pertinent comments in relation to a case study on management:

The case study type questions in Section A are intended to test candidates' ability to relate theoretical knowledge to the situations described. The four main sources of error were:

(a) Failing to absorb, or ignoring, the information given. Each item of information in the situation should be carefully considered, its relevance to the question determined and its implication deduced.
(b) Making assumptions about missing information. As in real life, the information is usually incomplete. Students must avoid unsubstantiated assumptions but should take into account uncertainties.
(c) Some of the conclusions drawn from the information were so absurd that it can only be assumed that the candidates have studied or revised a limited number of topics and convinced themselves at first glance that the case is about one of them. The information is then distorted to fit this view.
(d) Misinterpretation of the information. The question revealed a number of areas where candidates appear to have difficulty in relating practice to theory.

Examine the facts

Some analysis, classification, reclassification and interpretation of the facts may be appropriate and necessary to help you arrive at worthwhile decisions. When case studies are complex, it is difficult to keep all aspects of the problem in mind at once. The span of attention is only between five and nine items, and you should therefore group data to keep it within this. Use mind maps, tables, graphs, algorithms, diagrams and flowcharts, as appropriate, for this.

Apply problem-solving techniques where applicable, such as ratio analysis, decision trees, discounted cash flow, marginal costing, breakeven analysis, gap analysis, growth share matrix, directional policy matrix, SWOT analysis, the product life cycle and so on.

Application of the organization and methods questioning approach (purpose, person, place, sequence and means) discussed earlier in this chapter may give you a greater insight and facilitate closer analysis of the problem. Display to the examiner that you can integrate and apply the concepts, knowledge and theory from your course to the practical requirements of the case study.

SWOT analysis is particularly suitable for analysing a case study written around a particular company. The strengths and weaknesses of the company can be identified as part of the analysis of its internal characteristics. Strengths are distinctive competencies that a company has in relation to competitors, and might include a unique product, skilled employees, and superior research and development, marketing and financial expertise.

Weaknesses are the aspects of the business that do not measure up favourably in relation to competitors. These might include obsolete technology, lack of managerial leadership, poor industrial relations, and dissatisfied staff.

Opportunities and threats are factors external to the company. An opportunity is a chance to follow a new strategy that could be of benefit to the company. This might be an opportunity to exploit new technology, develop a new product or new markets, or produce previously patented goods where the patents have recently expired.

Threats are events that may prevent a company from meeting the needs of its customers or achieving its mission, or may ultimately threaten its existence. Threats can include new competitors entering the market, adverse trends in interest and foreign exchange rates, or proposed legislation (such as taxation increases by the government) that may hinder the financial viability of the company. Threats can often be turned into opportunities if anticipated and guarded against.

Develop alternatives

This is the creative stage of the problem-solving sequence. One source of inspiration should be your own experience. This may be from your own work experience in an organization, your leisure-time experience of being a member of a voluntary or professional organization, or your everyday experience of dealing with other organizations as a customer. How would these organizations solve the problem?

Novel solutions, provided they are sensible, acceptable and practical, may also win you good marks. Brainstorming and lateral thinking are well-known methods for coming up with original ideas. Use a Mind Map to get your ideas down on paper and to show the interrelationships between different ideas.

In specialized fields, such as financial accounting, management accounting, financial management, management, economics, strategic planning and marketing and so on, there are well known tried and tested standard procedures, techniques and models for solving problems. For example, in marketing you might use the product market strategies of market penetration, market development, product development and diversification.

In addition, you might consider positioning, segmentation, niche, marketing mix and pricing strategies for different stages of the product life cycle. In management, you might consider delegation, improving the span of control, reducing the number of levels in the scalar chain, encouraging team spirit, improving controls, training and development, and so on.

In strategic management, you might consider organic growth or growth by acquisition (horizontal, vertical, concentric or conglomerate). Other strategies might include joint venture, franchising, divestment, corporate venturing or a management buyout.

Pick the best alternative(s)

Having considered the alternative strategies that the company should pursue, pick the best alternative. Obviously, there are many alternative solutions to any problem. Therefore, you should rank alternatives in terms of their benefits. Look at the pros and cons of each, and eliminate the impractical and less profitable. Risk and uncertainty should also be taken into account. Qualitative outcomes of solutions should be considered.

The criteria for the best alternative should include cost–benefit analysis, practicability, and acceptability of the proposed solution to the case study under examination. What is the effect on the bottom-line result? To be worthwhile, the overall profitability, effectiveness and efficiency of the organization should improve.

Implement the solution

Describe how you would do this in practice, through a plan for implementation – for example, via delegation, training and development, improved communication channels, counselling and reorganization. List the types of problems, constraints and obstacles that may be encountered and need to be overcome in practice when an attempt is made to sell and implement the solution – for example, limited resources of staff and time, staff resistance to change, trade union objections, company policy and so on.

When will implementation take place? How will it be done and who will do it? How much will it cost? What might be the corporate, financial, production, personnel, marketing, organizational, behavioural, customer and competitive implications of implementing the strategy? What contingency plans should you make to overcome likely problems?

Monitor and follow up

Monitor and follow up to see that the implemented solution has proved to be as successful as intended, and also to learn from problems encountered and shortcomings highlighted. Say how you would do this in practice.

Remember, the management of time is just as important when answering case studies as when answering more conventional examination questions.

The three main faults in answering case studies

In an examiners' report for a major professional body, the examiner mentioned three main faults exhibited by candidates in answering case studies:

1. Wasting time by restating the information given in the question.
2. Failing to draw conclusions that logically followed from the information.
3. Making totally unjustified assumptions about the situation described – which in turn is likely to lead to quite irrelevant answers.

Tips on presentation

If the story of the Creation can be told in 400 words,
if the Ten Commandments contain only 297 words, if Lincoln's immortal
Gettysburg Address was only 266 words, if an entirely new concept of freedom
was set up in the Declaration of Independence in about 1,300 words –
it is up to some of us to use fewer words, and thus save the time, energy,
vitality, and nerves of those who must read or listen.

Jerome P. Fleishman

Learning objectives

- Why is presentation so important?
- What are the basic rules of good presentation?
- How can I apply these rules to gain more marks in the examination?

Importance of presentation

All the professional examinations and university degree programmes now highlight the importance of presentation. In the rubric to one major accountancy body's examinations, the following is stated:

Answer the question using:

- effective arrangement and presentation;
- clarity of explanation;
- logical argument;
- clear and concise English.

Similarly, the other professional bodies are placing greater emphasis on written presentation skills. The development of all-round presentation skills is important in most professions. The next section deals specifically with the basic rules of good written presentation.

Effective arrangement and presentation

Break up your answer into paragraphs. A paragraph is a group of sentences forming an idea. Answers may have anything from three to ten paragraphs or more. For effect, you should vary the length of your paragraphs. Drop a line between each paragraph for better visual presentation. Also, signpost each paragraph with a title (i.e. the key idea). Paragraphs should be developed and sequenced in a logical order which demonstrates to the examiner that you are working to a plan.

The first sentence of your paragraph is the topic sentence. This indicates clearly what the paragraph is about and helps you stick to the point. Now develop your main point by explanation, elaboration, analysis, illustration and example.

The subject matter of your paragraph should be organized in a coherent and concise manner. Points within each paragraph should flow and evolve logically and naturally from the ideas presented.

Your final paragraph should be an effective conclusion following logically from the preceding paragraphs. Indecisiveness is not the hallmark of a professional. Mere summarization is a waste of time and will win you no further marks.

As appropriate, use headings, subheadings, indentations, underlining, listing and numbering of points within answers to enhance presentation.

Remember, there is nothing more irritating to the eye than one long, unbroken, homogeneous answer. The examiner is put off even before reading the script. Hence the importance of paragraphing.

Clarity of explanation

Develop an individual style

Writing is a creative process, so develop your own style. Avoid trite or well-worn phrases, which should have no place in an examination. Thinking in terms of the reader means adapting your style and the content of your answer to the examiner's requirements.

In presenting a case, write impersonally and authoritatively. Avoid saying 'I think that' or 'in my opinion'; it is better to say that 'some management theorists consider that'. Be objective; your political opinions or views are not required. A layman's answer is not good enough. The examiner wants you to demonstrate the fact that you have read the required books, reflected on issues, and followed the recommended course of study.

Meaning

An ambiguous word or sentence is one that is open to a number of interpretations. You should therefore choose the appropriate technical word for the job. Be sure that your answer makes sense.

Try to visualize yourself as the examiner, and imagine how you would react to the script if you were examining it. After all, the examiner is an expert in this area. Therefore, the precise technical language of the discipline should be used as appropriate. This highlights the importance of building up your vocabulary of the technical terms used in the subject area. These are the building blocks that you need to help you write with clarity and precision.

Grammar

In addition, apply the main rules of grammar and use words in their correct sense. Good punctuation will help make your sense completely clear. Two people can only understand each other if they use words and phrases that belong to accepted good English.

To quote from an economics examiner:

Sometimes sentence construction is so bad, or explanation so confused, that it is impossible to determine what the candidate is trying to say. What cannot be interpreted cannot be marked.

Logical argument

Problem identification

Accurate identification of the problem, proper analysis and succinct presentation of conclusions are all required for successful professional work. Therefore, answers must be structured and logically thought out. Point B should be developed and follow logically from point A. Concepts, arguments, theories, ideas and practical implications should be organized and linked in a logical sequence.

Follow question structure

The answer should follow the structure implicit in the question. Underline the key words in the question before beginning your answer, and incorporate these key words into your answer to show the examiner that you have read and clearly understood the question. Technical terms should be defined comprehensively to help you develop your answer. Avoid contradictions and unsupported statements which do not follow from the facts presented.

Lengthy, undisciplined, repetitive answers containing wild speculation and invalid assumptions will suggest to the examiner that little time has been spent thinking about the question and its implications. This not only wastes valuable time, but also gains few marks. Relevancy is the key to success in answering exam questions.

Conclusions should be derived logically from the case made. Candidates should never assume that points will be inferred from their answers; they should, instead, always explain fully the development, source and reasons for their thinking.

Clear and concise English

Clear and precise

Clarity of mind is usually evidenced by clarity both in speech and in the written word. On the other hand, a student's lack of understanding is often camouflaged by verbosity and long-windedness. Precision and clarity of expression will prevent misrepresentation and misinterpretation. Words have different shades of meaning, so be sure to use those which communicate precisely the meaning intended. Finally, remember the four Cs of good writing: clarity, correctness, conciseness and coherence.

Be concise

Why use many words when a few will do the job just as well? The examiner who is working to a deadline does not have all day to wade through your padded material. After all, there are hundreds more scripts to get through and he or she only gets paid the same fee for each.

The examiner will normally strike out pages of verbiage and waffle. Non-answers in the form of tautological statements such as 'Accrued expenses are expenses which have been accrued' are wasteful of time and will earn no marks. Therefore, be selective in the points you make and the words you use.

Why, therefore, make the job more difficult for the examiner than it has to be? The solution, of course, is to be brief, clear, simple, legible and direct. Brevity has been defined as words that cover more ground than they occupy. Get quickly and directly to the point. The following are some examples of verbose phrases and the suggested shorter equivalents:

Verbose phrases	Concise phrases
In the normal course	normally
In view of the fact that	because
In the near future	soon
At the present time	now
In spite of the fact that	although
Make a revision	revise

To quote an examiner:

Candidates often lacked the ability to express themselves concisely and consequently wrote at length in expressing a single point.

Keep your sentences short

Clarity does not automatically follow on from brevity, although, generally speaking, being brief does enhance clarity. Bear in mind, however, that you can be too brief as well. A happy medium is desirable. Therefore, vary the length of your sentences. This puts variety in your style and makes your writing thoughtful, interesting and pleasing to the eye. On the other hand, being long-winded is often synonymous with confused and woolly thinking.

Readability

Dr Flesch, author of *The Classic Guide to Better Writing* (Flesch and Lass, 1996), recommends that the average sentence should be about 17 words long. If your sentences are more than 20 words long, you should beware. Experts also recommend that you should keep your word count to at least 70 per cent one-syllable words for greater readability. Readability then is determined by the choice of words used, the length of sentences and the clarity and conciseness of expression. This is not always practical when technical terminology is appropriate, but is nevertheless a good guiding principle to abide by.

Good spelling

Professional examinations are not a test of spelling. However, good professionals, as well as being able to express themselves, should also be able to spell. For example, to quote an economics examiner:

Spelling mistakes abounded: aspiring managers should not be writing entrapreneur, competative, oppertunity, shoping, comodity, summerized and suppermarket – all examples from the current scripts.

The following words are commonly misspelt.

Correct spelling	Often misspelt as
Accommodation	Accomodation
Beginning	Begining
Competence	Competance
Definition	Defination
Feasible	Feasable
Interrupted	Interupted
Relevant	Relevent
Separate	Seperate
Successfully	Sucessfully

You should also try to avoid confusing principle with principal, access with assess and so on. Make your own list of problem words that you frequently misspell or confuse with other words. Study and eliminate these mistakes from your life once and for all time. Acquire and use a good dictionary to help you in your efforts.

Summary

Presentation skills are very important for potential accountants and other professionals. Good presentation skills can make the difference between a pass and a marginal failure in examinations. It therefore pays to develop your presentation skills. The following form the basis of good presentation skills:

- Effective arrangement and presentation
- Clarity of explanation
- Logical argument
- Clear and concise English
- Good spelling
- Legible handwriting.

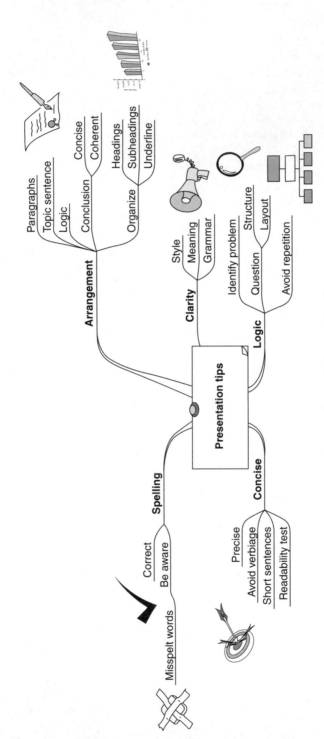

Mind Map of Chapter 8: Presentation tips

Reports, assignments and dissertations

What is conceived well is expressed clearly, and the words to say it will arrive with ease.

Nicolas Boileau.

Learning objectives

- How can I structure a report?
- What is the best way to research a dissertation?
- What is the best structure for a dissertation?
- What do examiners look for in a dissertation?

Reports and assignments

As part of your examination, you may be required to write answers in the report format. As a practising accountant you will be asked from time to time to provide reports on a variety of topics, including budgets, tax, investment appraisal, feasibility studies, cost savings, profitability and operational issues.

As part of a degree programme, you may be required to do written assignments or projects that are expected to follow the report format. Assignments are usually between 2000 and 3000 words in length. The general approach is similar to that of writing a thesis, but the requirements are not as rigorous. Well-written reports have the following structure:

- *Title page.* This should include the title, date, reference, number, classification (confidential or otherwise), author's name, who commissioned the report, and to whom the report is to be sent. For academic reports and assignments, this will be the college the student is attending. The title should be centred, bold and in larger font. White space increases the visual impact.
- *Executive summary.* This is also called the abstract. It should include the purpose and scope of the report, method of investigation, findings, conclusions and recommendations.

It should be about one page in length. It is usually located at the front of the report, and will help readers decide whether or not they need to read the complete report. An executive summary is only necessary if your report is long.

- *Contents list.* A report of more than a few pages should have a contents list giving page numbers. Use the headings and subheadings of your report to draw up the list of contents. A following page, where appropriate, may include acknowledgements to those who have assisted the author. Courtesy also demands that you acknowledge the ideas of others.
- *Introduction.* The introduction should include the terms of reference, brief history of the topic, reasons for the report, who the report is for, limitations of the report, treatment of the subject and special considerations.
- *Body of report.* This should include the method of investigation, concepts used, evidence collected, evaluation and the detailed findings. Use bold font to make headings stand out. Use headings for main sections and subheadings for associated themes. Use bullet points or indent lists as appropriate. Italics can be used to highlight important information.
- *Findings.* Findings should be itemized and categorized.
- *Conclusions.* Conclusions should be consistent, reasonable, logical, clear, concise, itemized, discrete, and fully considered. Conclusions should be supported by well-researched evidence. No new evidence can be introduced at this stage. They should logically follow on from the findings.
- *Recommendations.* Recommendations should be sound, sensible, well defined, concise and itemized, and follow on logically from the findings and conclusions. No new discussion, concepts or evidence can be introduced at this stage.
- *Appendices.* Place information that is not essential to understanding your findings but supports your analysis in an appendix. Appendices may include statistical tables, detailed results of surveys, questionnaires, graphs, a summary of results from elsewhere, correspondence, quotations, maps, photographs, bar charts, flowcharts and diagrams. Appendices should be numbered so that they can be easily referenced within the body of the report.
- *Glossary.* If there are a lot of technical terms and abbreviations in the report, a glossary is necessary.
- *Bibliography and references.* This is a list of books and articles consulted during the preparation of the report or assignment. The Harvard system of referencing is recommended. Citations in the text of the report or assignment should be as follows: Smith (2001). Where there is more than one author, you need only give the name of the first: Smith et al. (2000). The bibliography should be in alphabetical order and should include the name of the author, date of publication, title, edition (if not the first), place of publication, publisher, page number and volume number as appropriate.

Effective report writing

Before you write:

- Plan your report in the form of a Mind Map. Use the Mind Map initially to structure your ideas and later on to structure your thoughts.

- Be clear what your purpose is. What are you trying to achieve?
- Identify the information you want to get across.
- Bring together the resources, such as notes and references, that you need to do the writing.

During the writing:

- Write straight through the first draft. You can fine-tune the report later on.
- Arrange your material in a logical sequence.
- Structure the report using sections, headings and numbered paragraphs.
- Make the layout and content user friendly.
- As you write, keep the readers' needs in mind all the time. The report should engage the readers from the start, hold their attention, and win them over by the soundness of your arguments and the logic of your conclusions.
- Be clear, direct and concise. Short words and sentences aid clarity. Rephrase unwieldy sentences and eliminate unnecessary words. Break 30-word sentences into two or more shorter sentences.
- Choose the right words for the job. Use concrete words rather than abstract words. Use technical words as appropriate. Avoid acronyms, but if you feel they are necessary, explain them in the glossary.
- Avoid repetition and irrelevancy. Eliminate redundancies and the overuse of particular words or phrases.
- Do a spell check. Do a proofread as well. Don't rely totally on a computer spell check, as it will not be 100 per cent accurate. Spell checks do no pick up omitted words or the use of a wrong word spelled correctly.

After the writing:

- Check your work. Check for grammar, punctuation and spelling. Attention to detail is one of the primary traits of a professional accountant.
- Get a reliable colleague to read it and give his or her honest opinion.
- After a few days, reappraise your report with a fresh eye. Put yourself in the reader's shoes. Is it easy to read and has it a coherent structure?

The order of writing is really a matter of taste, but the following order for writing the report is suggested:

- Body of report
- Findings
- Conclusions
- Recommendations
- Introduction
- Appendices
- Glossary
- Executive summary or abstract
- Bibliography and references.

Dissertations

All the professional accountancy examinations now give exemptions for relevant business diplomas and degrees. Students may be exempted from all stages except the final one. Many diploma and degree programmes, in addition to written examinations, require students in their final year to do a minor dissertation of around 10 000 to 15 000 words.

A dissertation gives students the opportunity to identify a topic or a line of argument and to support their insight with relevant systematic questions. The following is a brief overview of the approach that should be adopted when preparing your dissertation.

Research model for a dissertation

The following provides a brief overview of the research process:

- Define problem
- Review literature
- Formulate hypothesis
- Research design
- Implement
- Interpret
- Report.

Define the research problem or question

A problem well defined is a problem half solved. You need to avoid getting the right answer to the wrong question. The research must help isolate and identify the problem to ensure that the real problem, rather than a symptom, is investigated. Formulate your initial research question, research objective and research proposal. Constructing a research question will give you a sharper focus to your work. It is important to choose a question that your review of the literature will help you answer.

Research objectives will help you to specify and clarify the information you'll need. For the research project to be successful, the research problem must be converted into clear and precise research objectives. The research proposal is a written statement of the research design drawn up to investigate the research question, and will allow your tutor to evaluate your proposed research and see if any changes are needed. Most research proposals will include purpose of the research, research design, data-gathering techniques, budget and time schedule.

What is your initial hypothesis? A hypothesis is your tentative proposition, which you will need to verify through further investigation. It acts as a guide to the researcher, as it suggests the method to be followed in studying the problem. In many cases hypotheses are hunches or theories that you have about your research question.

Review literature

Review the literature to see what is available to support your hypothesis. Carry out a preliminary review of books, magazines, newspapers, research reports and the Internet.

Use your librarian to carry out a search of relevant databases. Do these support your hypothesis? The purpose of the exploratory research is to narrow the scope of the research progressively and nail down specific research objectives. It will also show how feasible the research project is. Are there sufficient resources accessible to support your ideas?

Formulate your hypothesis

Formulate or reformulate your hypothesis, based on the findings of your initial research. Firm up your research question, research objective and research proposal.

Research design

This comprises two aspects: the literature review and the empirical research. Both are very important aspects of your work. You will now research the literature pertinent to your research question. The empirical research will be done in-company to support your thesis.

Implement

You can carry out the literature research and empirical research concurrently, or as opportunity presents itself. In any event, you should be doing one or the other at any one time. It is important that you are constantly making progress towards your goal of completing your dissertation.

Empirical research may involve designing questionnaires, interviewing staff or studying archival information in the company. In relation to your questionnaire, pilot questions to test their appropriateness and objectivity. Write as you go. You need to keep complete records of everything you do as you do your research. Don't rely on your memory!

Interpret

You will probably need to analyse the information collected and classify it in the format that best suits your purpose. Tables, graphs, bar charts, pie charts, diagrams and flowcharts may be useful. You will need to draw up findings, conclusions, and recommendations based on your literature and empirical research. How do the two match up? See to what extent the literature research findings are corroborated by your empirical research.

Report

This is your dissertation, and should follow accepted practice and college guidelines as regards presentation and layout. A typical layout would be:

- Abstract
- List of contents
- List of tables and exhibits
- Introduction
- Literature research
- Empirical research
- Main body giving analysis and discussion

- Findings, conclusions and recommendations
- Bibliography.

What examiners want

Generally, examiners want you to display competency in the literature and empirical research, presentation and layout, and in your findings, conclusions and recommendations. Overall, your dissertation should be carefully organized and properly referenced. More specifically, examiners are interested in the following.

Abstract

This should include the research question, the research methods used, and a summary of the findings, conclusions and recommendations.

Introduction

The introduction should give the reader a clear idea of the central issue of concern in your research and why you thought that this was worth studying. It should incorporate a full statement of your research question and research objectives. It should include a 'route map' to guide the reader through the rest of the dissertation. This will give brief details of the content of each chapter and present an overview of how your story line unfolds. The introduction usually is fairly brief, but it is very important.

Body

This should show logical development. The material chosen from the literature review should be relevant and support your purpose. It should demonstrate that you have read widely to find information to back up your thesis. It should include the debates and arguments on your chosen subject.

Your empirical research should be well thought out, sensible, practical, and support your thesis. You should defend the reasons why you chose a particular approach or research methods and give reasons for rejecting alternative methods. You should give the advantages and disadvantages of the chosen method. Theoretical models may be drawn on to justify your thesis. Generally, your work should show creativity, insight, sound judgement, innovation and originality.

Findings, conclusions and recommendations

This is probably the most important part of your dissertation and deserves the most attention when preparing. Together with the abstract, it may be the only part of your dissertation that is thoroughly read. Point out how your empirical findings agree or disagree with the findings of your literature research.

This section should highlight the significance of your findings, conclusions and recommendations. You should demonstrate an understanding of the organizational constraints and practical implications that may affect your findings. Your recommendations may also suggest areas for further research.

Drawing up the research proposal

- *Title*. This may change during the course of your research. Initially it should mirror your research question. Keep your topic narrow and focused.
- *Background*. This should state why you think your research is necessary. Set out the research question and why it has aroused your curiosity.
- *Research question and objectives*. These should leave your tutor in no doubt what you are trying to achieve.
- *Method*. This is the research design and data collection approach. This will show how you hope to go about your research. The research problem should dictate the research method. State where you are going to do your empirical research, and who the research population is going to be. State what research techniques you are going to employ, such as interviews, questionnaires, statistical techniques, examination of company records or any combination of techniques. Issues of access and ethics should be addressed.
- *Time scale*. Build in buffer time, as research always takes longer than anticipated.
- *Resources needed*. Consider time, finance, data access and equipment. Expenses may be incurred for travel, subsistence, help with data analysis, or postage for questionnaires. Make sure you have access to data needed to do your research. You will need a computer to analyse data and compile your dissertation, and also to access the Internet.
- *References*. You should give a page or two of references. You must give the impression that your initial literature review has been reasonably thorough. The references must be directly relevant to your research question. Use the Harvard system of referencing.

A suggested research time scale

This is an estimate of how long each stage of the process will take. It highlights the need to plan each stage of your work and have time deadlines for each stage. The following is based on a dissertation where you have six months to complete the job, and is suggested for guidance only:

- Complete research proposal and agree it with your tutor in month 1
- Carry out initial literature review during month 1
- Define research questions and objectives during month 2
- Draft literature review during month 3
- Design empirical research during month 4
- Implement empirical research during month 4
- Write up the empirical research and do the analysis during month 5
- Produce first draft of dissertation during month 6
- Submit dissertation at end of month 6.

Preparation of dissertation

Prepare an outline of your dissertation early on. A good way of doing this is to prepare your list of contents, which is the map of your proposed dissertation. The appendices, bibliography and list of illustrations can be done in between other jobs. Multi-tasking is the approach to adopt.

Use index cards to take notes as you do your research. Use Mind Maps to brainstorm and organize your thoughts. Write up your findings as you go along. When you have completed your research, the actual writing-up process will be much easier if you have kept comprehensive records in a systematic way. Record full details of sources needed to compile your bibliography. Compare and contrast what different authors have to say about your thesis.

The physical elements of your dissertation will include a hard cover with title, a similar page just inside the cover, an abstract, list of contents, list of illustrations, main text, appendices, bibliography and a glossary, if necessary.

Use tables, charts, diagrams, models and maps, as appropriate, to illustrate your dissertation. Maps may be used to show the layout of factories, offices and so on. Make sure your illustrations add to your work rather than detract from it.

A formula for writing analytically

1. State your argument/thesis
2. Summarize what others have said:
   - Source A
   - Source B
   - Source C etc.
3. Offer a comparative analysis:
   - Discuss similarities
   - Discuss differences
4. Compare empirical with literature research
   - Discuss similarities
   - Discuss differences
5. Summarize and draw conclusions.

Writing the abstract

The abstract, together with the findings, conclusions and recommendations section, is the most important part of your dissertation. It is probably the only part that some people will read, so it is important that it gives an accurate representation of the main work.

Generally, the abstract should be about one page in length. It should be objective, precise and easy to read.

It is difficult to write a good abstract. Some people wait until the end of the dissertation to write the abstract. Others write it tentatively at the start as it gives a brief overview of the thesis. You can always change it as you progress or at the end of the dissertation. The abstract should stick exactly to what you have written in your dissertation. It should convey the content of your thesis in as clear and brief a way as possible. The abstract is not the place for elaboration or adding new ideas.

The abstract should provide the following:

- The research question
- Its importance
- The research methods employed
- Summary of findings, conclusions and recommendations.

The abstract can be a separate part of your dissertation, placed in a separate section before the main body of your work.

The layout of the rest of the dissertation will vary from individual to individual, but one suggested layout might be as follows:

Chapter 1	Introduction
Chapter 2	Research methodology – empirical research
Chapter 3	Research methodology – literature review
Chapter 4	Synthesis of literature review
Chapter 5	Content analysis and empirical research findings
Chapter 6	Findings, conclusions and recommendations

Divide chapters into sections so that you have enough organizers to give a clear structure to your work. Divide sections into paragraphs. Within paragraphs you may use bullet points as appropriate.

Summary

A typical report will have the following:

- Title page
- Executive summary
- Contents list
- Introduction
- Body
- Findings
- Conclusions
- Recommendations
- Appendices
- Glossary
- Bibliography and references.

   A similar approach is often adopted for academic assignments.
A research model for a dissertation may have the following approach:

- Define problem
- Review literature
- Formulate hypothesis
- Research design
- Implement
- Interpret
- Report.

Examiners want a minimum of:

- Abstract
- Introduction
- Body
- Findings, conclusions and recommendations.

A research proposal should have the following:

- Title
- Background
- Research question and objectives
- Proposed research method
- Timescale
- Resources needed
- References.

   A suggested research time scale is given in this chapter, and a framework for analytical writing suggested. Vital tips on the preparation of a dissertation are also given.

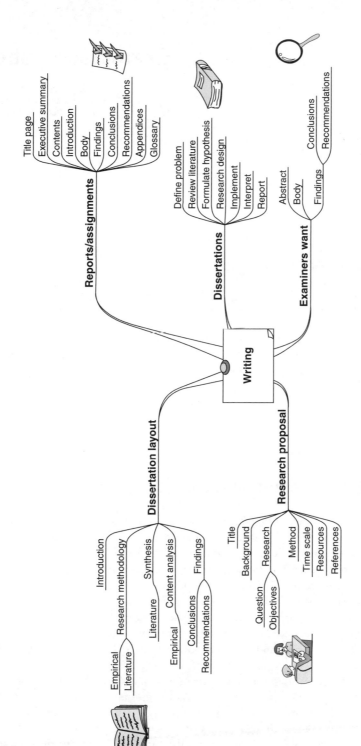

Mind Map of Chapter 9: Writing

Examination stress

The mind is its own place, and in itself can make
a Heaven of Hell, a Hell of Heaven.

Milton

Learning objectives

- What is examination stress?
- How does it affect my concentration and performance in examinations?
- What coping strategies can I employ to counteract and control examination stress?

What is examination stress?

Stress can be thought of as an individual's response to threats and challenges in the environment. It can be manifested psychologically or physiologically, or both. It is the way an individual reacts to and handles stress that determines whether it is good or bad.

Examination stress results from the potential threat to self-esteem, such as loss of face, which might arise with exam failure. This is caused by individual perception of the gap, whether real or imagined, between the difficulty of the examination and an examinee's capabilities, or the difference between an individual's existing state of knowledge and the desired ideal.

Some additional anxiety can be brought about through lack of examination preparation and practice. For example, a candidate may not have covered the syllabus adequately and be afraid that something not covered will come up.

Less able people become more anxious as exam time draws near than those who are more able. The latter group tends to see examinations as less threatening. It is quite likely that the more significant the examination is to the career prospects of the candidate, the more seriously it will be perceived, resulting potentially in higher levels of anxiety. Parents, fellow students, lecturers and employers can also transmit their anxiety to students, thus exacerbating an already tense situation.

Students who have failed an examination on a previous occasion are likely to be more apprehensive and anxious before a resit because they do not wish to go through another humiliating experience. The danger here is that students may be subconsciously conditioning themselves to feeling anxious for all examinations. It is important not to allow such behaviour patterns to develop into permanent ones, thus becoming part of a person's personal baggage.

The good news, however, is that most students forget their anxiety as the examination gets under way. The physical action of writing and the mental activity of concentrating on the here and now reduces stress.

Effects of stress

Psychological

Psychological responses include apprehension, self-doubt, forgetfulness and poor concentration. Unreleased built-up tension can contribute to health problems such as high blood pressure, coronary heart disease, hypertension and cancer. So it pays to combat anxiety not only for examinations but also in your lifestyle generally.

Excessive worry can have adverse effects on academic performance. The process of preparing for and taking examinations is, for most people, a stressful affair. Stress often increases as examination time approaches. A certain amount of anxiety is normal. It keeps the adrenalin flowing and may in fact sharpen your concentration powers, thereby improving your examination performance.

A high level of anxiety may affect concentration to such an extent that examinees fail to note important examination instructions, such as the number of questions and the choices available. This is a common complaint from examiners. In open-book examinations examinees have even been known unintentionally to mix up their scripts with their books and take them home. However, the appropriate amount of stress can actually help memory, provided it is short term and not too severe.

Stress facilitates the production and delivery of glucose, making more energy available to the brain's neurons. This in turn improves memory reception, retention and recall. However, if stress is prolonged, it can impede the delivery of glucose to the brain and disrupt memory.

There is obviously an optimum level of anxiety. A high level is stressful, and hinders concentration, intellectual control and examination performance. A low level is unstimulating and causes lethargy. This has been recognized in the psychological law called the Yerkes–Dodson Law. This states that anxiety improves performance until a certain optimum level of arousal has been achieved. After this point, performance deteriorates.

Physiological

Bodily responses to stress include increased heart rate, shortness of breath, trembling hands, shaking legs, palpitations, nausea, sweating, pallor and in some cases fainting. Physical signs such as increased heart rate, increased blood pressure, fatty deposits in the blood and perspiration can be measured scientifically.

High levels of anxiety can also cause physical symptoms such as sleeplessness, headaches, aches and pains, lack of appetite, listlessness, stomach pains and even vomiting.

Coping strategies

Coping strategies include examination technique, mental approaches, and those related to lifestyle.

Examination technique

Practice

Plenty of mock examination practice over a period of time will help to build up your tolerance levels for stress. This will acclimatize you to potential stressful examination situations and thus help you to counteract them. Anticipation of the forthcoming examination increases the level of anxiety, which will be at its worst just before the examination starts. Therefore it is important to keep your imagination under control, for example by creative visualization, as examination time approaches.

The mind cannot accommodate two thoughts at the same time, so whenever a negative thought enters your head, substitute a positive one for it. You can be as positive as you make up your mind to be.

Establish a routine

Follow an established, rehearsed routine at the beginning of the examination. Practise calculating the time allocated to each question in relation to the marks awarded, the routine of reading the instructions, reading the questions, choosing the ones you are going to attempt and drafting outline answers. Practising this routine in your imagination is just as effective as if done in reality. Develop this skill so that it becomes an automatic response. Then, when the real thing happens it won't bother you. On the principle that forewarned is forearmed, anything which reduces uncertainty and indecision will help control worry.

Overlearning

Some examinees say that their minds go blank inside the examination room. This is probably because they haven't learned the material thoroughly enough. Mastery of the subject matter to the point of overlearning reduces anxiety because the examination is now perceived as being less difficult. Students who are ill prepared are bound to worry. On the other hand, students who are well prepared actually enjoy and thrive on the experience, which only helps them peak at their maximum performance in the examination room.

Creative visualization

Mentally train for your examinations. You can practise taking examinations successfully in your own imagination. Rehearse in detail in your own mind the steps involved as a dry run. Psychologists have found this is practically as good as doing the real thing. Athletes use creative visualization in addition to their normal training to enhance their overall performance. For example, this is an important aspect of a professional boxer's training. In sport it is now accepted that psychological training is just as important as physical training.

Study and examination technique

Developing good habits in this area, such as time management, concentration, effective reading, memory, Mind Mapping and presentation skills, will help to optimize your performance and reduce worry.

Set yourself realistic goals

Setting yourself the goal of becoming a professional basketball player if you are only 5 ft (150 cm) tall would certainly be unrealistic. Similarly, if you are very tall it is unlikely that you will make a successful jockey. Have regard to your strengths and weaknesses in setting goals. There is no point in trying to qualify as an accountant, or indeed in any other profession, if you do not possess the appropriate aptitudes and necessary dedication.

Unless you have considerable time, energy, willpower, commitment, application, aptitude and intelligence, trying to complete each stage of a professional accountancy exam in six months may prove a very daunting and stress-provoking objective. However, some exceptional people have achieved it. So, unless you are one of these gifted persons it would be better to leave twelve months for each stage and pace yourself accordingly.

Success first time around will reinforce your confidence and motivate you for subsequent parts. Have long-, medium-, short- and immediate-term goals. An immediate-term goal might be to meet a revision session objective. Little successes create the proper positive mental set and thus build up your confidence.

Mental approaches

Motivation

If you are an intrinsically motivated student you will probably be able to handle worry better than if you are extrinsically motivated. The former type of student wants to pass the exam because of the wish to satisfy his or her own needs rather than the wishes or needs of others. The latter type worries about what people will think if he or she fails the examination. This creates further anxiety.

Models

Find out how successful examinees cope with stress in the examination room, and use them as models to modify your behaviour and control your anxiety levels. People learn by modelling themselves on the successful coping strategies of others.

Desensitization

Before the examination, think of the things that are likely to cause you anxiety. Now imagine yourself dealing with each of these issues successfully and conclusively in a cool, relaxed and competent fashion. Rehearse this creative visualization in conjunction with a relaxation technique over a period of time. When the actual examination situation comes round, you will behave in a less anxious way. You have learned a relaxed, comfortable association with a situation that previously caused anxiety and even panic.

Positive thinking

Self-preoccupation and negative thoughts should be avoided. Think of ways in which problems can be solved and difficulties surmounted. Think positively and constructively. Practise positive self-talk rather than negative. Negative self-talk lowers performance and increases worry; positive self-talk has the opposite effect.

Positive thinking will therefore eliminate worry and enhance examination performance. Say to yourself 'I'm going to pass this examination', rather than 'I'm hopeless at exams'. Rehearse in your mind, through creative visualization, positive experiences of past examination successes and other achievements. Keep these positive thoughts in your mind. Think success.

Reframing

Reframing is looking at something from a different viewpoint, seeing it in a new context. Good learners anticipate good positive outcomes. However, it you do fail a subject, see the failure as a learning opportunity. Analyse the reasons for your failure and take corrective action to ensure success in the future. Learn from your mistakes. Occasional setbacks should strengthen your resolve to be successful next time round.

Laughter is the best medicine

Develop a sense of humour. Laughter often provides new perspectives on stressful problems. Laughter is therapeutic. It can relax nerves, improve digestion and help circulation. Learn to laugh at yourself and at life. Try to see the humorous side to life. Watch your favourite comedy on TV and relax. Surround yourself with happy people. Avoid the continuous complainers.

Persistence

How many times have you seen students just get up in the middle of the examination and leave? You have no chance at all if you give up so easily. Develop your willpower and determination. You should enjoy utilizing your willpower and going all out to be successful at your exams. Say to yourself, 'My willpower keeps getting stronger. I enjoy using my willpower. It feels good to go all out.' Stick to the task. Give it your best shot.

If during the examination you have not done as well at a paper as you thought you would, do not give up. It is possible that other candidates found the going just as tough. Be positive about your performance, and concentrate on achieving excellence in the next paper.

Meditation

Meditation is a technique to quieten your mind. Practise clearing your mind of disturbing thoughts. A simple but effective technique is to imagine a calm place to control your stress levels. Meditation means sitting quietly and focusing your attention on one thing at a time, such as your breath, a candle flame, a prayer or a mantra.

Meditation is a type of distraction. It is based on the principle that you can't meditate and worry at the same time. Meditation slows down your brain waves to an alpha state of 8–13 cycles per second. Meditation can bring you to a state of deep relaxation called the serenity zone. It decrease stress, anxiety and depression. It is claimed that meditating for as little as 20 minutes once or twice a day confers significant benefit.

Confidence

This is an individual's belief in his or her own ability. For examinations, it is the expectation of a successful outcome. Build on your success. Nothing succeeds like success. Failure situations should be avoided. Success reinforces the expectation of success and thus lays the foundation for further achievement. Thus, if you are inadequately prepared for an examination, do not sit it.

Concentration

This is focused attention or strong thinking activity directed at a limited area so that other areas are simultaneously shut out. Build a wall of concentration around you. Concentrate on the here and now; forget about the past and future. You want to shut out everything except the topic under study. You must become so absorbed in what you are currently doing that you become completely unaware of all other potential distractions. Think about the task rather than about yourself.

Improve concentration through positive self-talk. Developing concentration powers in the examination room must also be learned and practised. Self-talk such as 'I'm beginning to concentrate', 'I'm now concentrating fully' and 'my mind is crystal clear' will condition the mind in the appropriate way. Remember that in the examination room disciplined concentration powers of up to three continuous hours' duration are required.

Lifestyle

Relaxation

Use techniques such as meditation, breathing exercises and progressive relaxation methods. Progressive relaxation works by sequentially tensing and relaxing muscles from head to toe. Adopt a comfortable sitting or lying position for these tension-reducing exercises.

Various forms of breath control can be practised anywhere, and help to reduce stress. For example, a well-known breathing exercise is taking a deep breath, holding it and then breathing out – all done in the ratio of 1 : 4 : 2. This simple exercise reduces anxiety by optimizing oxygen and carbon dioxide levels in the blood. If you want to pursue these ideas further there are many books and cassette tapes available on relaxation techniques.

Listening to your favourite music can also be a great way to unwind and induce a state of relaxation. Likewise, reading a favourite novel can be relaxing.

Health

Sleep, exercise and eating wisely are all ways of keeping a sound mind in a sound body. Vigorous exercise will help you sleep soundly, and a balanced, varied diet with adequate fibre will combat stress and fatigue. Eat plenty of fresh fruit as part of your normal diet.

Some medical experts recommend that you should drink eight glasses of water a day (dehydration thickens the blood while hydration thins it) and reduce your salt intake as part of any stress management programme. Make sure that you regularly get at least eight hours' sleep. If you can get by on less you are exceptional.

Leisure time

Many students worry when preparing for professional exams, while a tiny minority suffer severe mental stress. A good recuperative antidote to the stress of preparing for and sitting examinations is to have leisure-time activities built into your plan – 'All work and no play makes Jack a dull boy'. More than 2000 years ago Plato said:

Anyone engaged in mathematics or any other strenuous intellectual pursuit should also exercise his body and take part in physical training.

Obviously, the ideal leisure-time pursuits should be outdoors with plenty of fresh air and reasonably energetic in order to counteract the sedentary study time activity. Cultural pursuits, such as theatre and cinema, should also be part of your leisure-time activities. These will take your mind off exams and help you relax.

Support system

It is a good idea to discuss your worries with a trusted friend or family member. A sympathetic ear and a good listener are great antidotes to worry. Just having someone to confide in occasionally can be a great source of peace and comfort.

Some organizations provide a mentor support system for employees who are studying. If this is available to you, you should use the service. The role of the mentor is to advise, coach, coax, encourage, support, empathize with and generally assist learners. Mentors might be colleagues, supervisors or managers/employees who have themselves completed the degree or qualification being sought. Mentoring provides human contact and a source of support and advice when needed.

Mentoring also provides an opportunity to build lasting relationships with others in the organization, and this could aid your career development. There are certain advantages to having a supervisor or manager as mentor – among others, it will help you to stick to your studies. Being able to negotiate study leave with a sympathetic supervisor is an extra bonus.

Employees who have recently completed the examinations may also be willing to act as mentors. They have the added advantage of knowing the problems, pitfalls and anxieties of sitting the exams.

Alternative stress

Some psychologists feel that your leisure time should be sufficiently different and challenging to provide alternative stress. This should occupy your mind totally so as to counteract by distraction any possibility of preoccupation with study- or examination-related problems.

Leisure-time activities should be built into your programme as a way of rewarding and reinforcing good study practices. There is a positive correlation between physical fitness and peak examination performance.

Personality type

The medical profession has identified a particular type of person who is considered to be prone to stress and its related health risks. They have called this type of person the 'A' type. The person who follows a more moderate and less stressful existence they have named the 'B' type. The type A person is always in a hurry (hence the term, hurry sickness), forever trying to meet deadlines. The type A person is very competitive, always has to win and tends to be reactive.

The type B person, on the other hand, is more methodical and proactive, and is just as ambitious but goes about his or her work in a less aggressive but nevertheless systematic, purposeful manner. The type B student works to a plan, has developed good study skills and is aware of and practises good examination technique. Research has indicated that many chief executives are in fact type B. A good model for any ambitious student to imitate!

The type B person has established correct priorities, practises good principles of time management and as a result achieves the same goals with less hassle and energy output than the frenetic, nervous energy output of the type A person. The type A person is more prone to a host of illnesses, including stomach ulcers, cancer and heart disease, than the type B person.

From an examination point of view, some of the coping strategies outlined will not only help you to be more successful in your examinations but will also establish a more healthy, stress-free lifestyle for your future. If you want to live a long, happy and healthy life, then model your behaviour on that of the type B person.

Summary

Unmanaged stress lowers attention, concentration and intellectual control. Managed stress, on the other hand, can maximize your performance in the examination room. Coping strategies, which can be used to counteract and control examination stress, include:

- Examination practice
- Overlearning
- Desensitization
- Positive thinking
- Relaxation
- Meditation
- Creative visualization
- Lifestyle techniques
- Support system
- Having realistic goals.

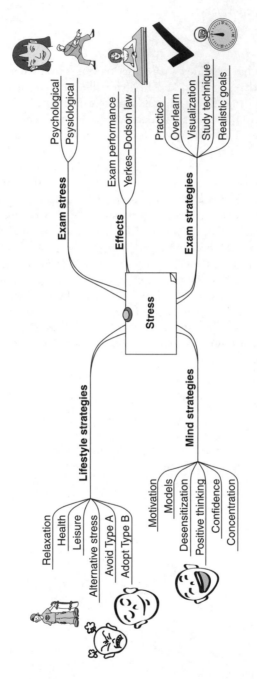

Mind Map of Chapter 10: Stress

Examination faults

Common sense is not so common.

Voltaire

Learning objectives

- What are the common examination faults?
- What are some of the specific exam faults in the computational and narrative areas?
- What steps can I take to improve my exam performance in these areas?

Common faults

Examiners often complain about the following faults, which are caused by, among other things, lack of proper planning.

Layout

Faults include:

1. Deleting phrases, sentences or paragraphs from a script. This looks messy and certainly creates a very unfavourable impression. Only do it if absolutely necessary. In this context, do not waste time on rubbing out or using white correcting fluid; instead, just delete the mistake and insert the correction overhead.
2. Inserting material, and the frequent use of detailed footnotes.
3. Putting a line through a whole section or page of an answer and starting again.
4. Leaving blank spaces in the middle of an answer, hoping for subsequent inspiration. Most examinations prescribe that you start each new question on a fresh page, so if you want to leave a blank space for subsequent inspiration why not leave it at the end of your answer?

5. Answering parts of the same question in several places of the answer book without guidance to the examiner. Remember, practices which make marking more difficult for the examiner are not to be recommended.
6. Failing to use paragraphs, subheadings and indentations as a good presentation technique.
7. Writing your script in pencil, which is not recommended as it may fade or smudge.

Irrelevancy

Faults include:

1. Giving global, generalized answers when specific information is required.
2. Failing to understand and answer the question set. This could be due to wishful thinking, incorrect reading or misinterpretation.
3. Writing pleading notes to the examiner to be lenient because the examinee's career will be in jeopardy if he or she does not get a pass. This says little for the maturity of the candidates concerned and only annoys the examiner. This may seem far-fetched, but some candidates do resort to such desperate measures.

Time management

Faults include:

1. Answering more than the number of questions required in the belief that the examiner will mark only the best of the answers. This is not so, and anyone who has time to answer extra questions will hardly do justice to the others.
2. Not leaving sufficient time to answer all of the questions required. There is a tendency to spend too much time on the first question attempted and too little time on the last.
3. Failing to distribute time in proportion to the marks given. Also, candidates often do not distribute their time within questions in proportion to the marks awarded.

Planning

Faults include:

1. Failing to plan answers before committing thoughts to paper. Quality not quantity is important. Verbosity is no substitute for clear, concise, logical thinking and good presentation.
2. Failure to plan – i.e. the candidate fails to look before leaping. It is important to read the question carefully and figure out exactly what the examiner is looking for before starting an answer.

Specific faults

For our purposes this section will be divided into two broad categories – computational or number-based subjects, and those that are narrative or description-based. The computational category includes accounting, quantitative methods, cost accounting, management accounting techniques, financial accounting, business taxation, management accounting and financial management. The narrative category includes economics, business law, information technology management, management, company law, control and audit and strategic planning and marketing. This classification is for convenience only; some subjects are both computational- and narrative-based. Therefore, some examination questions may require a combination of the two.

Usually the computational subjects require more study hours than the narrative-type subjects because of the need to develop the practical skills and technical competence required to gain exam standard proficiency. Mere reading of textbooks is not sufficient. For example, in an examiner's report, the cost accounting examiner stated:

Candidates who marginally failed this paper probably did so because they were not technically competent over the whole syllabus. It is obvious that some candidates (and possibly their tutors) deliberately omit part(s) of the syllabus from their study programmes; this is a dangerous practice which is not to be encouraged.

Computational subjects

Reasonableness

Candidates sometimes fail to check their answers to see if they are reasonable and based on common sense. Examiners are sympathetic to those who evidently understand the principles but who make small slips in arithmetic. They are, however, obviously much less sympathetic when ludicrous or impossible answers are given which could have been rectified if commonsense principles had been applied.

Balancing

In subjects like financial accounting, do not spend too much time trying to balance. Stick to a planned time allocation. You may still get excellent marks even though your balance sheet or cash flow statement doesn't balance. The approach, layout and application of concepts is much more important than arithmetical accuracy.

Workings

Some candidates fail to show intermediate workings when they use a calculator, but produce the wrong answer. A proportion of the marks for all questions is reserved for methodology. After all, the rubric will usually state categorically that candidates must clearly show how they have derived their answers from the basic data. They will lose marks if they do not do so even if their answers are correct. The examiner cannot read your mind. Marks will only be awarded for what is shown.

Interpretation

The explanation/interpretation aspects of computational questions are sometimes answered very badly. Some candidates are unable to explain principles which they can apply numerically. This suggests that would-be professionals and business graduates should spend more time developing their written communication skills. For example, in ratio analysis, as well as being able to calculate the relevant ratios you must also be able to interpret in words their significance in relation to the question given. Many candidates are competent at calculating the ratios, but when comparative figures are given are unable to interpret the results in a meaningful way.

Presentation

Presentation is a very important aspect of quantitative subjects. Good, clear, concise, logical and methodical presentation is expected, and marks are reserved for such. The examiner will award marks for apparent logical thinking and understanding even if the result of the calculations is incorrect. For example, budgets are not simply a mass of calculations but should be presented in a tabulated and logical manner. Sloppy layout, such as scattering figures in an uncoordinated way over several pages, is not going to endear you to the examiner.

Study model answers and published financial statements for good layout practices. A tabular statement or matrix can save you time and earn you extra marks. Appropriate illustrations such as diagrams or graphs can also be very effective – but do remember to label them clearly!

Arithmetic

Poor arithmetic, non-alignment of columns of numbers, careless positioning of decimal points and inaccuracy in simple multiplication are inexcusable for potential accountants and business graduates. Sometimes the inaccurate figures are used to support wrong and often ludicrous conclusions. In this context, correctness in basic computational techniques such as compound interest, graphs, bar charts, diagrams and percentages are an essential foundation.

Examiners also often complain that candidates are unfamiliar with the use of, say, mathematical tables for students. If your examining body advises use of a particular set of mathematical tables or another aid, ensure that you use it.

Published accounts

Study published accounts. This will give you a feel for the practical, real-life world, and make you realistic and less dogmatic when answering questions on the interpretation of accounts. It will familiarize you with the best presentation methods as well as the formats required by the Companies Acts and the financial reporting standards. You will also know what value-added statements are, and will not confuse them with profit and loss accounts or Value Added Tax.

Many published accounts also use bar charts, pie charts, graphs and other presentation techniques to illustrate their accounts. Study these to see the various methods and best practices now used to present and illustrate accounting data.

Integrated holistic approach

When answering questions, remember that all areas of your course, including previous stages, may be relevant. Don't put subjects into pigeonholes. Try to perceive the integrated nature of the course. Particularly at the latter stages of the professional examinations and business degree programmes, your ability to integrate knowledge from all areas of the course is examined. Case studies are particularly designed to bring out and test this skill.

Accounting standards

Know your accounting standards. It is foolhardy going into an examination of a professional accountancy body without knowing these thoroughly, particularly at the later stages of financial accounting.

Taxation

Good, clear, concise, neat and logical presentation with good figure work is essential for this subject. Taxation is a practical and very technical subject. Therefore, as well as having a thorough grasp of your subject you must be able to apply the knowledge to the problems set.

Tax is a technical subject requiring a good detailed and up-to-date knowledge of both taxation principles and law. To quote from a tax examiner's report:

Too many enter the exam hall knowing little about tax but with a determination to fill their workbook by making up the law as they go along.

Narrative subjects

Law

Law is a technical subject requiring a sound, detailed and precise knowledge of statute and case law. You must display to the satisfaction of the examiner, by the content of your examination script, that you have acquired, understood and can apply this body of knowledge. Common sense, generalizations and a layman's knowledge are not sufficient to pass examinations in law or indeed any other subject.

A person seeking professional advice would not appreciate a general reply that did not address the particular problem posed. Answers should be structured with this in mind. To quote from an examiner's report:

Very short answers necessarily attract few marks. The examiner wants discussion, reference to cases and statutes, and evidence that the candidate has thought about the question and is giving a reasoned answer rather than regurgitation of rote learning.

Report writing

Reports should be logically sequenced, structured and formatted correctly. They should have a title and a date, and should be addressed to somebody and from somebody. They should be signed at the bottom by the accountant or manager (do not conclude with phrases such as 'Kind regards' or 'Yours sincerely'). Reports should have paragraphs, headings, subheadings and indentations as appropriate, and should finish with a conclusion. Calculations, graphs and tabulations should be relegated to appendices.

Terms of reference and summary recommendations should be given at the start of the report. Conclusions should be logically developed and clearly stated. Examiners complain that students often write an essay when asked specifically for report format. (Refer to Chapter 9 for more detailed requirements for report writing.) In addition, it would be well worth referring to any book on report writing in business for guidance in this area.

Information technology management

This paper will test a candidate's real understanding, rather than any ability to reproduce rote-learned descriptions of some aspects of information technology. It is difficult to acquire this real understanding without practical hands-on experience. Candidates should therefore seize every opportunity to acquire practical experience of using computers, and keep up to date generally on information technology. With the spread of personal computers in most organizations, getting direct experience of computers should not be too difficult.

Spreadsheets

Some companies run in-company courses on computer appreciation, Excel, Lotus 1-2-3 and other software packages, as well as on keyboarding skills. Try to get a place on one of these. Take every opportunity to read computer magazines, and visit computer hardware and software exhibitions. Also, should you get the chance, visit other companies' computer installations.

Develop the skill of flowcharting if you want to do well in these examinations. You should also realize the importance of spreadsheets to accountants and managers in such areas as budgetary control, financial planning, cash-flow forecasts, tax planning and so on.

Economics

Economics is a real-life practical subject, the ramifications of which affect our everyday life. Economic topics such as interest rates, foreign exchange rates, taxation, balance of payments, gross national product (GNP), gross domestic product (GNP) and the government's annual budget are continuously being debated on the television and radio, and also in the daily press and financial journals.

However, the popular press approach is not sufficient for these examinations. Instead, read good quality newspapers and journals such as the *Financial Times* and *The Economist*. Show the examiner that you understand the practical implications and significance of what you are studying. Proving that your knowledge extends beyond the recommended texts will help you to impress the examiner.

Economics is the type of subject that lends itself to being illustrated by flowcharts, graphs and diagrams. Frequently, a diagram correctly drawn and properly explained is by far the best way to answer a question in economics. Some questions in fact cannot be answered without clear and accurate diagrams. An example is the relationship of costs and profits, and supply and demand.

Remember that it is technical knowledge that distinguishes the professional from the layman, and it is the ability to communicate that technical knowledge that will convince the examiner of your professionalism.

Management

The case study-type questions are intended to test candidates' ability to relate theoretical knowledge to the situations described. Draw conclusions logically from the information given. Do not make totally unjustified assumptions about the situation described; this will lead to irrelevant answers. The systematic approach to solving case studies recommended in Chapter 7 should be applied. Management has its own terminology, which you must get to grips with.

Summary

There is a number of basic little tips you can apply to specific subjects that will help you maximize your marks in the examinations. However, there is no substitute for adequate expertise gained from study and application of the subject matter. Most of the advice offered is common sense, but common sense is a rare commodity, judging from the regularity with which these points are addressed in the examiners' reports of the various professional bodies.

Common faults include:

- Poor layout
- Irrelevant answers
- Poor time management
- Lack of planning.

Specific faults include:

- Computational errors
- Unreasonable answers
- No workings
- Lack of an integrated approach
- Lack of technical knowledge.

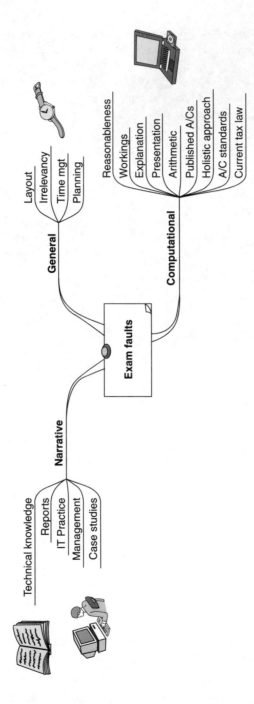

Mind Map of Chapter 11: Exam faults

Examination technique

Just as eating against one's will is injurious to health,
so study without a liking for it spoils the memory,
and it retains nothing it takes in.

Leonardo da Vinci

Learning objectives

- What should I be doing as examination day approaches?
- What is the best approach in the examination room?
- Why do people fail examinations?
- What is the best approach in answering multiple-choice questions?
- What are the four basic ingredients for examination success?
- What is the systematic approach to answering questions?

Preparation

You are now aware of and have been systematically applying study techniques, presentation skills and stress management techniques. Now plan your review:

1. Have a proper timetable.
2. Space your revision.
3. Variety is important – don't study the same topic all night. Alternate subjects to maintain interest and freshness of mind.
4. Recall and revise as indicated in Chapter 6.
5. Employ stress management strategies.
6. Tackle past examination questions, preferably under mock examination conditions. Remember, practice makes perfect.

Examination questions

Study old examination papers

See the number of papers there are in the examination. Study the layout of the paper. How many questions are there, and how much time is allowed? How many marks are allowed for each paper and for each question? Is there a choice of questions? Are there case studies? Do some questions require a report format answer? Will multiple-choice questions be set? Is computer-based assessment used for some subjects? All this should be known before you go into the examination room.

Be on the look-out for likely examination questions

Draw up a matrix of past topics in your subject to establish trends, if any. There are fashions in academic subjects just as in anything else. Study the relevant professional journals. For example, questions in the examination are frequently on topics featured in professional journals and professional student magazines. Sometimes, examiners base questions on these articles. Student magazines also feature good articles from time to time on study and examination technique, which are always worth perusal.

Pay particular attention to the business section of a quality newspaper or better still read *The Economist* or the *Financial Times*. These will often indicate current topics of interest in the financial world and may very well be the basis of examination questions.

Remember, examiners like to cover the whole syllabus in three to four sittings. Therefore, important examination topics which have not come up for the past one or two sittings are probably very likely to come up this time. However, don't take any chances. Cover the syllabus adequately as some questions require the application and integration of knowledge from all of the subject area as well as from more than one area of the overall syllabus. Just pay particular attention to these likely examination topics as the examination date approaches.

Revision

Attempt a mock examination

Sit a past examination paper if possible, and get feedback on your performance from your tutor. Devote two weeks before examination time to your private revision work. The more examination practice you get the better.

Consult your examination syllabus for the areas covered

More than 50 per cent of many professional courses is based on the higher cognitive skills such as conceptualization, analytical work, identifying and using appropriate techniques, interpretation of results and problem solving. There is now less emphasis than before on number crunching and memory and more on conceptualization, problem-solving and understanding; less emphasis on compilation of figures and more on interpretation of results.

Many professional institutes have published explanatory notes on the abilities required for their syllabus against each examination topic. Some provide estimates of likely times needed to study each subject. These are guidelines only, but nevertheless give some indication of the time required to get up to speed and acquire the necessary exam competence in each subject. These guides should help you decide how much study and revision time should be devoted to each topic.

Syllabus guidance notes

These notes have been prepared by examiners to assist lecturers and students in preparing for the examinations. They are revised frequently, and the latest version should be consulted. Some professional institutes publish these in their professional and student magazines.

Syllabus subject Mind Maps

It is important to study the syllabus very carefully. A Mind Map of each subject area should be drawn up so that you can see at a glance the range of topics to be covered. It can also be used as a planning and revision tool, items being marked off as they are being studied. Using this method, there is no chance that complex or unattractive topics will be overlooked.

Make sure that you have covered everything

Avoid re-reading textbooks, manuals or correspondence course notes at this stage. Stick to the Mind Maps, summary Mind Maps and cue cards, and revise definitions, rules, case law and formulae. Study past exam papers and solutions, especially for areas likely to come up in your exams.

The day before

You should use the day before the examination for preparation and a last revision of your Mind Maps or notes. Do not attempt to learn new things at this stage. This last round-up revision will strengthen your memory for the forthcoming event. Do not overdo the revision. Two hours browsing through your Mind Maps should suffice. Go to bed at your normal time. Put your examination equipment in your pocket, including pens, rulers, watch and calculator, so that you will be organized in the morning, and don't forget your watch!

Examination centre location

Find out where the examination hall is

Dry-run the route in advance so that you know exactly how long it will take you to get there. Build in a contingency allowance for possible traffic hold-ups. Determine the exact location of the room where the examination is going to be held.

Last minute revision

Arrive at the examination centre in plenty of time. Use your summary Mind Maps and cue cards to flash through key concepts, definitions and mnemonics. This will bring the points to the front of your short-term memory. You can capitalize on this (the Recency Principle of Memory) when you are inside the examination room. When you get inside the examination room, write down as much as you can remember. You may be able to use this information during the examination. However, do not attempt to bring cue cards into the exam room with you.

It is inadvisable to discuss examination subject-related topics with colleagues beforehand or during the progress of the examinations at lunch break. This may cause confusion of ideas, and any anxiety and lack of confidence they may have may be transmitted to you. Putting doubts and uncertainties in your head at this stage may adversely affect your performance in other papers. Instead, avoid others to keep your brain crystal clear to maximize your concentration powers in the examination room.

Examination day

In the examination room, stay relaxed and confident. Remind yourself that you are well prepared and are going to do well. If you find yourself anxious, take several slow, deep breaths to relax. Inhale deeply for five seconds and exhale for the same amount of time.

When you receive the paper, make sure that you read it from beginning to end. Before this, provided you have the opportunity while the invigilator is handing out the papers, write in your examination number on as many of the sheets of stationery provided as possible. This saves vital minutes later on and gets you a little bit more organized for the task ahead.

Read the instructions to candidates carefully

Decide what each question requires. Organize the order of the answers. Answer your 'best' question first, making sure you do not spend too long on it in relation to the marks available, then tackle your 'second-best' question and so on. Remember you need not answer the questions in the numerical sequence given on the question paper itself. However, when finished you must put them in numerical sequence before you hand them in.

Your examination paper may contain a mix of long and short questions. Don't fall into the trap of assuming that length correlates with difficulty and thus avoid doing the long questions. In fact the converse is often true.

Answer the question asked

Do not produce some figment of your imagination. You must demonstrate a sufficient breadth and depth of knowledge as well as understanding to pass third-level examinations. You cannot do this adequately if you repeat the same information in different answers, even if the questions given appear somewhat similar.

Budget your time

Do not ignore whole sections or spend too much time on one small section. Allocate time to each question in proportion to the marks given. Not answering all the questions/sections required shows the examiner that you have not covered the syllabus adequately, that you were banking on certain parts of the syllabus coming up or that you did not allocate your time properly in the examination room. Leave 10–15 minutes at the end of the paper for review and checking.

Candidates who take a chance and confine their study to a restricted area of the syllabus will almost certainly fail in any degree or professional examination.

When answering questions, concentrate on the main issue. Do not be afraid to display as much relevant knowledge as possible. Support your points with relevant examples from your work experience. This is a very effective way of demonstrating knowledge and, in professional examinations, is one of the things the examiner is looking for. Theory is not much use if it can't be related to practice. One example to support each point is sufficient.

Plan your answers

In practice, it has been found that most students tear into their answers and write straight-away.

Plan your answers for better presentation and more marks

Make an outline Mind Map of the main ideas in your answer. Most examination questions are looking for answers with seven or eight points. Structure your paragraphs around these points. Use headings, subheadings and indentations to clarify your answers. Number and underline the headings for emphasis. A well laid-out answer will make the examiner's job easier and win you extra marks at the same time.

For questions requiring a discussion, have an introduction, a middle (development of the theme) and a proper conclusion. Introductions should be short. It is better to get to the core of the question quickly. Sometimes a good diagram properly explained is the best way to answer an examination question (a picture speaks more than a thousand words). However, do not waste time by duplicating the information by words if the diagram is self-explanatory.

Adopt useful time-saving devices such as using initials or standard abbreviations of the subject, providing you explain the term or terms fully when introduced.

Write simply and to the point

Watch the following: grammar, spelling, punctuation, handwriting, paragraphing, layout and neatness. From an examiner's point of view there is nothing worse than script that looks like Chinese when it is meant to be English. The examiner is not going to waste valuable time trying to decipher the hieroglyphics. It is better to write less in an answer legibly than it is to write quickly and illegibly. So write clearly. Failure to do so will lose you marks, as the examiner cannot award marks for something that cannot be read. Finally, if you finish early do not leave the examination room. Stay and check your answers until the time allowed is up.

Advantages of planning

If you do not plan, your answer will present the examiner with pages of unrelieved and homogeneous script rather than proper signposted and paragraphed material. During the answer, do not rephrase the facts of the problem stated in the question. This is a complete waste of precious examination time. Without planning you are more likely to wander all over the place and repeat points already made. Repetition using different phraseology does not fool the examiner.

Another advantage of planning your answers instead of writing non-stop for three hours is association. Ideas will often come to mind when planning the answer to one question which will help in answering another. However, don't rely on your memory; jot down the ideas as they come to mind. Your answers will more than reward the little effort and planning time expended. After all, the examiner has built a thinking time allowance into questions. Therefore, you are expected to think and reflect about the issues raised in the question. You cannot do this if you are writing all the time.

Planning will prevent you from attempting questions for which you have insufficient knowledge. Thus time-wasting, panic reaction, and switching to and fro between questions will be avoided. During the answering of questions you will also be less likely to become confused if working to a plan.

Causes of failure

For the average intelligent student, the causes of failure have been identified as:

- Inadequate motivation and poor concentration (the approach to study)
- Bad study technique (studying itself)
- Poor examination technique (exhibiting the results of study).

It has been observed that success in most exams depends on a combination of:

- Inherent intelligence and special abilities
- Effective study and examination techniques
- Chance – the topics you have studied, or are good at, might just come up on the day!

Therefore, the chances of success are significantly greater for those who have been exposed to (and practised) proper study and examination techniques than for those who haven't. Finally, remember there is no substitute for hard work. Study techniques will only make the road a little easier; they won't get you through the examination on their own. You need an excellent grasp of the subject matter to pass the relevant papers. Genius has been defined as 1 per cent inspiration and 99 per cent perspiration – so don't rely too much on your inspiration when examination time comes along!

Why examiners fail candidates

The following are summarized highlights of why examiners fail candidates. A little time invested by students in reading a few examiners' reports should pay handsome dividends. After each cause of failure, some tips are given on how the problem can be overcome.

Preparation

Many students are totally unprepared for the examination. Examining bodies are dedicated to maintaining high standards. Many business students, particularly those studying professional rather than degree courses, both work and pursue part-time studies. Such students consequently won't have as much time for study as, say, the average full-time arts student who generally has 15 hours in class each week and studies for about 25 hours – a total of 40 hours devoted to academic work. Someone who spends anything up to 40 hours or more at work needs to clock in at least another 20 hours in private study and classroom work.

Students' performance in examinations is directly correlated with the amount of time, application and effort put in. If you follow our advice, your study time will be both productive and effective.

Presentation

Examiners often state that presentation is slovenly or of a standard quite unbecoming to an aspiring professional or graduate. Develop good presentation skills. Study the layout of suggested answers. In your working life slovenly work is likely to be returned to you for correction, modification or improvement. Similarly, such work in examinations is unacceptable.

Answer the question set

The questions answered by candidates are sometimes unrelated to what is printed on the question papers. Read the questions carefully. *Pay particular attention to the 'requirement' section*. Realize that every word is important and means what it says, and that extreme care has been taken by the examiners to ensure clarity. Look for key or limiting words, and use these to set the scope and limits of the question.

Use the questioning technique. What is the question about? What exactly does the examiner want to know? Decide on the broad idea of the subject matter the question deals with, and then converge on the particular aspects that are required. Make sure your answer is relevant to the question as a whole. As you write the answer, stop occasionally and check that your answer is consistently relevant to the question asked. This self-monitoring will prevent you straying away from the point.

Time management

The ability to work within time limits is an important element of a manager's work. It is also an important aspect of university degree and professional examinations. Poor usage of time in the examination hall has resulted in question papers not being finished in the time allowed.

Allocate your time in proportion to the marks given. For a three-hour paper, this works out at 1.8 minutes per mark. Therefore, for a question with 30 marks you should allocate 54 minutes (1.8 × 30). Five minutes of this time should be reserved for planning, and a few minutes should be set aside for review. Spend approximately 46 minutes actually doing the question.

Apply the same approach to each question. Reserve a few minutes at the end of your examination to review your entire script quickly. Only add things at the end if, as you reread, you see that important conclusions are missing. If you run out of time and there is still one question unanswered, you could very well get some marks by outlining briefly how you would have answered the question.

The law of diminishing returns

This law operates in relation to examination answers. The first 50 per cent of the marks for any question are much easier to get than the last 50 per cent. Similarly, the first few marks on a question are relatively easy to get, whereas the last few are extremely difficult to earn. Thus it is easier to score a few marks on a question which at first sight you thought you knew little about than spending more time on a question that you know a lot about and have already done justice to. This highlights the importance of attempting all the required questions.

Balanced answers

You should write approximately the same length of answer to each question. For example, writing four pages of script for one question as against one for another shows either poor time management or a detailed knowledge of one topic and a superficial knowledge of another. Similarly, an unbalanced answer in which some sections receive too much attention shows a lack of planning or judgement and an inefficient use of time.

Write something

If you write nothing you cannot gain marks. Candidates who write something relevant will usually gain some marks. These marks could turn a borderline fail into a pass. Go into the examination determined to succeed. Give every question your best shot, even if you feel you know very little about the topic.

Breadth of knowledge

Remember that examiners are looking for breadth of knowledge over the whole syllabus, not depth of knowledge in a narrow field. Therefore, spending too much time on a favoured topic at the expense of others may cost you a pass. Time is also wasted by doing rough answers and then copying them out.

Keep up to date

Many students are unaware of recent relevant legislation, which results in outdated answers or outmoded layouts. Therefore, make sure that your textbooks are the most recent editions and that your notes are current. Purchasing secondhand books, while saving you money in the short term, could prove a poor investment in the long term. Also, watch the financial press, business magazines, accountancy press and, in particular for accountancy students, accounting and student journals for new developments.

Multiple-choice questions

In a multiple-choice examination, the student is required to select the correct or best response from several options. Items consist of a stem in the form of an incomplete statement, diagram, question, calculation or task to be solved. You must pick the correct response (called the key) from the options given. The incorrect responses are called distracters.

There are two basic kinds of multiple-choice questions. In one an incomplete statement can be combined with various options to make a complete statement which is either true or false. In the other a question is followed by various statements, one of which must be chosen as the correct answer.

In a quantitative question, a problem may be followed by various numerical options. You will need to do some quick calculations in order to find the right option. Check that your calculation is correct, as distracters incorporate common student errors.

Objective testing is now a popular form of examination. Answers are either right or wrong. Multiple-choice questions are the most popular form of objective test and are now used for some examination papers. The following approach to answering multiple-choice questions is suggested:

1. Read and heed the instructions. How much time is allowed? How exactly are you told to complete the answers? The latter is essential if the tests are computer scored.
2. Work through the whole paper. Answer those you find easy now. You can return to the more difficult questions later. Mark these on the margin with a question mark.
3. Highlight key words to ensure that you read and understand them fully.
4. Pick your best alternative – that is, the one you feel is nearest the correct answer. Eliminate those you feel are incorrect. This will limit your choice and at the same time increase your chance of getting the right answer.
5. Don't procrastinate. You need to get through the test within the time constraints set. Time management is, therefore, of the utmost importance.
6. Return to the more difficult questions. On rereading, the answer may come to mind. Where you don't know the answer, use logic and common sense. Random guesses are seldom correct. However, make sure you answer all the questions, as you are not penalized for wrong answers.

Computer-based assessment

Computer-based assessment (CBA) is now an accepted part of university degree exam programmes. CIMA and the Institute of Chartered Accountants in England and Wales are just some of the professional bodies that have introduced CBA for subjects in the foundation stages of their examinations. These are objective test questions produced on a computer screen, and are designed to test students' knowledge of a particular subject.

The advantages of CBA are that:

• Assessments can be done continuously rather than at the usual six-monthly intervals, thus allowing you to progress to other stages of the exam at your own pace

- Instant feedback of results is available on screen
- If you are unsuccessful you can re-sit the exam again when you feel you are ready.

CBA can be taken at accredited centres. Arrange with the CBA centre a date and time to take your assessment, and find out how much it will cost. CBA works as follows:

- Questions are displayed on a computer monitor
- You input their answers directly on screen
- You usually have two to three hours to complete the test
- The computer marks the answers when you have completed it
- You will receive your results on screen as soon as you finish the assessment.
- CIMA students who are successful receive a Certificate of Achievement and their exam status is automatically updated
- Unsuccessful candidates are provided with feedback on their areas of weakness and can use this information to concentrate on the areas of the syllabus that need their attention.
- You can arrange a re-sit as soon as you feel ready.

CBA may require you to do the following:

- Fill in a blank or blanks in a sentence
- List items in rank order
- Give a definition
- Identify a key issue, term or figure
- Calculate a specific figure
- Complete gaps in a set of data where the numbers can be derived from the information provided
- Identify required information on graphs or a diagram
- Match items or statements
- Answer true or false statements
- Write brief explanations to given data.

Tips for taking CBAs

In addition to the advice on multiple choice questions, you should keep the following in mind before taking computer-based assessments:

1. Practise past computer based assessment tests, such as those contained in texts like the CIMA Study System or other reputable texts.
2. Like any exam, know how long you have to complete the test, what the pass mark is, and what marks are awarded for. Pay particular attention to the instructions for completing the CBA.
3. Spelling may be important. CBA simply cannot cope with an infinite variety of spelling errors and so it is your responsibility to spell correctly.
4. Practise on longer, process-type questions. Studying conventional exam questions will help you how to apply knowledge and get used to the methodology and process involved in reaching a solution. These skills are necessary if you want to progress to further stages of your exams.

5. Be aware that CBA includes a range of question styles such as multiple choice, true/false, fill in the blanks, matching pairs of text and graphic, sequencing and ranking, labelling diagrams, state a definition, and that these will be used for testing as appropriate. You should be aware of and practise the different styles of questions before taking the test.
6. If you are doing the CIMA CBA, try out the demo online in order to get a feel for the technology involved. You need to know which buttons to press and when to press them, and which buttons not to press and when not to press them. In addition, it is useful to download past objective test questions from the paper-based exams for exam practice.
7. It is a good idea to talk to fellow students who have already done CBAs in order to get their advice on the process of taking such exams and the type of things that can go wrong.

Four basic ingredients for success

In the Report of the Examiners of a major professional body, certain basic ingredients for success (equally applicable to any course of studies) in the examinations are recommended to candidates:

1. Follow an appropriate course of study.
2. Practise answering past questions, and be fully aware of the rubric to each paper.
3. Get your tutor to criticize your work during practice sessions, since only feedback of this nature can help you monitor your progress and remedy your shortcomings.
4. Plan your approach to the answering of the questions. Enter the examination hall not only armed with full knowledge but also prepared to make full use of every moment of examination time. If only three-quarters of a paper is completed, then only three-quarters of that paper's marks are available.

With regard to the second point above, students should be aware that for some professional exams, booklets of suggested answers are written by members of the examining panel. Students should study these to try to gauge the examiner's philosophy and see exactly the type of presentation, style, standard, content and emphasis the examiner expects.

Solutions are not normally published for university degree programmes. However, undergraduates might benefit by working out the solutions themselves or by studying the equivalent subjects published by the professional bodies.

Examiners are human

Examiners are not ogres. They want you to pass the examination, but not at the expense of diluting standards. They have taken the examination themselves, so they do empathize with you. However, do not write notes pleading to the examiner for leniency. This is irritating to the examiner, a sign of immaturity, and a waste of your time.

Just like you, examiners get irritated and bored. Marking papers can be a tedious job at the best of times. They try to mark them in a conscientious, fair and honourable fashion. They would prefer to see you pass than fail.

To keep the examiner satisfied, interested and favourably disposed toward you, you should at least follow the rubric instructions and write legibly. If the examiner can't read what you have written, then he or she can't award the appropriate marks.

Examiners know their subject, they can't be bluffed, and they understand English. They are not interested in your pet theories, prejudices, religious beliefs, political opinions, moral judgements, social comment, biases, hatreds and so on. All they want is pertinent knowledge, facts and theory related to the questions set. They take the most rational, sensible and logical interpretation of the questions set, and mark accordingly. Great care is taken in formulating questions, and they are checked and rechecked to ensure clarity and precision of words.

To pass you must reach a good standard in each paper as well as achieving a good over-all standard. Some professional exam bodies publish explanation grades and band of marks covered by each. These are well worth consulting.

Systematic approach to answering questions

Develop the habit of going about answering questions in a mentally disciplined way. The following general approach is suggested.

Read the question

First concentrate on what you are required to do, as indicated at the end of the question. Then read all of the question a few times until you have the gist of what is required. Note any special requirements, such as list, detail, advise, explain, report and so on:

- When asked to list or outline, do not give an essay
- When asked to summarize, do not give examples
- When asked to report, a report format is required.

Failure to follow examination instructions will lose you marks. (Refer to the appendix for a glossary of terms used in examinations.)

Think about the question

Think and reflect on the issues raised for a few moments. 'Stop and think' should be your motto.
Question:

- What does the examiner want?
- What is the subject area generally concerned with?
- What are the fundamental issues behind the question?
- What are the facts pertinent to the issues raised?
- How can I present them in a clear, concise, lucid and logical fashion?

Plan

Draw a Mind Map of the key points to answer the question, and then ask yourself again if these points are truly relevant to the question asked.

Answer

Use the key points of your plan as captions and write a paragraph around each. Stop after every few paragraphs and recheck that you are being consistently relevant and are not straying from the point.

Use a deductive approach (make an inference from general theories to the particular problem posed). This is in preference to an inductive approach (where students try to draw general conclusions from specific examples or, indeed, personal views).

Remember

Examinations are tests of theoretical knowledge. Theory may be illustrated by practical relevant experience. This is recommended, as it shows that the candidate can relate theory to practice. However, inventing your own theories, which is what you are actually doing by drawing general inferences from your own practical experience or personal views, is not acceptable to examiners.

The examiner requires evidence in the form of well-balanced arguments supported by reference to authors, books, articles and research studies, and also radio and television documentaries.

Review

Quickly review your answer, picking up misspellings, incomplete or nonsensical statements, lack of conclusions and so on. Apply logic to calculations. Check that they are within the parameters of the 'ball park' – figures which you should have precalculated on a commonsense basis for comparison as to reasonableness.

Move

Move on to the next question and start the process all over again.

Summary

You should have a systematic examination revision plan in operation during the last two weeks before the exam. Get past examination questions with model answers and work through them. Make sure you master frequently recurring topics.

In the examination room, read right through the examination paper – making sure you look at both sides of the sheet and see all of the questions. Allocate time to each question in proportion to the marks given, and spend about five minutes planning your answer before attempting the question. Make sure you undertake all the required questions.

Apart from lack of inherent intelligence, the reasons why people fail examinations are lack of proper motivation, poor study, and sloppy examination technique. The following are some of the basic reasons for failure:

- Inadequate preparation
- Poor presentation
- Failure to answer the question set
- Bad time management
- Failure to keep up to date.

A suggested approach to multiple-choice questions and computer-based assessment is outlined in the chapter.

The four basic ingredients for success are:

1. Follow an appropriate course of study
2. Practise answering past papers
3. Get feedback from your tutor
4. Plan your answers.

Remember, examiners are human. However, they do need your co-operation to help them get you through the examinations. So watch your layout and follow the rubric. Use a systematic approach to answering questions, as follows:

- Read the question carefully
- Think about the question
- Question the question
- Plan your answer
- Answer the question
- Review your answer
- Move on to the next question.

GOOD LUCK IN YOUR EXAMINATIONS! YOU CAN DO IT!

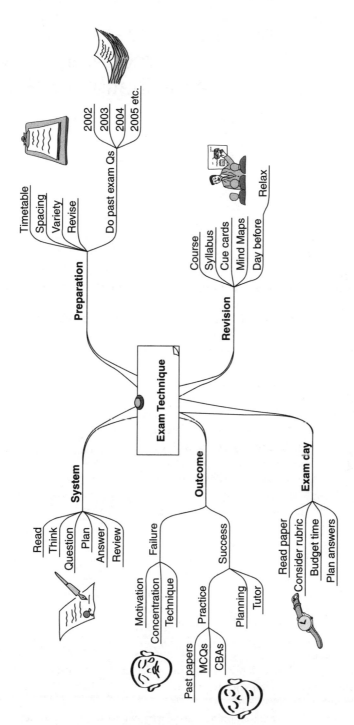

Mind Map of Chapter 12: Exam technique

Appendix: Glossary of terms frequently used in examination questions

Advise/recommend Present information, opinions or recommendations to someone to enable the recipient to take action.

Amplify Expand or enlarge upon the meaning of (a statement or quotation).

Analyse Determine and explain the constituent parts of.

Appraise/assess/evaluate Judge the importance or value of.

Assess See **appraise**.

Clarify Explain more clearly the meaning of.

Comment (critically) Explain.

Compare (with) Explain similarities and differences between.

Contrast Place in opposition to bring out difference(s).

Criticize Present the faults in a theory or policy or opinion.

Demonstrate Show by reasoning the truth of.

Describe Present the details and characteristics of.

Discuss Explain the opposing arguments.

Distinguish Specify the difference between.

Evaluate See **appraise**.

Explain/interpret Set out in detail the meaning of.

Illustrate Use an example – chart, diagram, graph or figure as appropriate – to explain something.

Interpret See **explain**.

Justify State adequate grounds for.

List (and explain) Itemize (and detail the meaning of).

Prove Show by testing the accuracy of.

Recommend See **advise**.

Reconcile Make compatible apparently conflicting statements or theories.

Relate Show connections between separate matters.

State Express.

Summarize State briefly the essential points (dispensing with examples and details).

Tabulate Set out facts or figures in a table.

Bibliography

Acres, D. (1988). *How to Pass Exams without Anxiety*. Northcote House Publishers.

Allen, C. (1972). *Passing Examinations*. Pan Books.

Buzan, T. (1974). *Use Your Head*. BBC Publications.

Buzan, T. (1993). *The Mind Map Book*. BBC Publications.

Davis, D. (1986). *Maximising Examination Performance, A Psychological Approach*. Kogan Page.

Easton, G. (1983). *Learning from Case Studies*. Prentice-Hall.

Flesch, R. and Lass, A. H. (1996). *The Classic Guide to Better Writing*. Harper Collins.

Gagne, R. M. (1977). *The Conditions of Learning*. Holt-Saunders International.

Gelb, M. J. (1988). *Present Yourself*. Jalmar Press.

Hanson, P. (1988). *The Joy of Stress*. Pan Books.

Kellett, M. (1980). *Memory Power*. Sterling Publishing.

Lorayne, H. and Lucas, J. (1976). *The Memory Book*. Starr Books.

Maddox, H. (1967). *How to Study*. Pan Books.

Malone, S. A. (1992). *Better Exam Results*. CIMA.

Malone, S. A. (1995). *A Critical Evaluation of Mind Maps in an Adult Learning Environment*. Dissertation submitted for MEd degree of the University of Sheffield.

Malone, S. A. (2000). *Learning Skills for Managers*. Oak Tress Press.

Norfolk, D. (1987). *Executive Stress*. Arrow Books.

Shone, R. (1984). *Creative Visualisation*. Thorsons.

Rowntree, D. (1970). *Learn How to Study*. McDonald.

Russell, P. (1979). *The Brain Book*. Routledge and Kegan Paul.

Wingfield, A. (1979). *Human Learning and Memory*. Harper and Row.

Index